IS
YOUR
CHILD
GIFTED
?

IS
YOUR
CHILD
GIFTED
?

A Handbook for Parents of Gifted Preschoolers

ELIZA BROWNRIGG GRAUE

Oak Tree Publications, Inc.
San Diego, California

Illustrated by Dave Graue

Published by Oak Tree

Distributed in the United States by
Oak Tree Publications, Inc.
San Diego, California

Library of Congress Cataloging in Publication Data

Graue, Eliza Brownrigg.
    Is your child gifted?

    Bibliography: p.
    1. Gifted children—Identification.   2. Child
rearing.   I. Title.
HQ773.5.G7   1985   649'.155   84-20633
ISBN 0-86679-007-1

First Edition
1 2 3 4 5 6 7 8 9 88 87 86 85
Printed and bound in the United States of America

To Dave, who walked with me

CONTENTS

PREFACE

During my teaching career, with both gifted children and others, I quickly came to appreciate the importance of those events that take place in the earliest years of a child's life. The attitudes and values students brought from home made some of them so eager to learn, so easy to teach! Clearly, the parents of preschoolers—especially gifted ones—have a crucial role to play in their children's education and the nurturing of their full potential.

As a parent of three gifted children, I share with many of you the frustration of "knowing" you have a gifted child but not knowing if you should be doing more or less about it, of being hesitant to share the joys of raising a special child for fear of being thought of as boastful, of the need to press for attention to be paid to the fundamental requirements of a child who happens to be exceptional in some areas, and of trying to find teachers who understand that average accomplishments can sometimes be a sign that something is wrong.

Now that my own children are grown, I still look back and wish there had been a single source I could have consulted on the problems and joys of parenting a gifted child. **Is Your Child Gifted?** was written to be that source book for you. Its purpose is to provide information about gifted children and their needs so you, the parent, will be able to make informed decisions concerning this venture: the nurturing of your gifted child. It examines the problems unique to the rearing, or parenting, of a gifted child, focusing primarily on early childhood (the preschool years) and concentrating on the nurturing of exceptional intellectual and creative-thinking abilities. Parents who seem to have no problem encouraging a child's artistic talent, athletic prowess, musical ability, or outstanding social skill somehow feel less sure of their competence in coping with intellectual precocity. It shouldn't be this way. This book can help you gain the confidence to do what you, more than anyone else, are most qualified to do: encourage the healthy growth of your own child in all areas of development.

If you have looked at the Table of Contents, or have flipped through this book, you found that we also touch on some subjects that do not appear to apply directly to the preschool child—topics that relate to the formal education of the gifted. Matters such as gifted programs, teachers, and testing are included because they become a concern of many parents who, realizing that their preschooler might have unusual intellectual abilities, start to wonder if the schools will be able to meet his special educational, social, and emotional needs.

You are not alone. Other parents are going through the same things you are going through now or have already had similar experiences. Before the first word of this manuscript was typed, many such parents were consulted for their advice and opinions as to the types of problems parents of gifted children might face and the kinds of information that would be useful to you. Their opinions and observations guided the selection of materials to be included in this handbook. **Is Your Child Gifted?** will, I hope, answer many of **your** questions, while providing both a sense of what is normal behavior for gifted children and the reassuring knowledge that others do share your concerns.

I am convinced that a parent with knowledge of gifted children and the factors affecting their development will be able to do a more effective job of parenting a gifted preschooler.

My apologies to the reader who might find my use of the generic "he" offensive. I find "he/she" and "his and hers" are not only awkward to write but distracting to read, and switching back and forth from he to she causes confusion.

My special thanks go to the students, faculty, and parents of the Pine View School for the Gifted in Sarasota, Florida, for their help and support, and to all the parents who read and responded to the various stages in the development of this book.

EBG

IS
YOUR
CHILD
GIFTED
?

Beginning and end shake hands with each other.

German proverb

1

Roots and Wings

When you selected this book you probably had some preconception about the meaning of the word gifted. But you may not have been so sure about the meaning educators attach to it or if they would use it to describe your child. Let's find out.

The term gifted is commonly used by educators to describe a small part of the large group of exceptional children, specifically those who are at the other end of the spectrum from those with physical or mental handicaps. It is a broad term that, unfortunately, implies a value judgment about the goodness of giftedness and the badness of handicaps. It also suggests a certain passivity—that some children, through no effort of their own, happen to have a capacity to excel that others do not have. Although there is a bit of truth in this attitude, it can be very misleading to those who live with the gifted. The truth is: **Most gifted people work hard to develop whatever advantage they do have.** As a result, differences that may not have seemed so great in early childhood have the potential of becoming extremely obvious later in life.

There probably have always been some individuals more gifted than most of the people around them. These persons of exceptional ability appear in all parts of the world, in every culture, and at all social and economic levels. Some are recognized early in life as prodigies, while some genius, because of the times or social circumstances, may never be discerned. It is hard to imagine how Madame Curie would have expressed her great ability had she been born centuries earlier in a tribal society. And what kind of recognition was given those ancient metal workers who developed methods of producing bronze? The work of such geniuses led humankind out of the Stone Age. We can only speculate how their ability would be manifested in today's world.

WHO ARE THE GIFTED?

When an individual displays an artistic talent, he is normally referred to as an artist; musical ability, a musician; psycho-motor ability, an athlete; someone with unusual social skills or leadership ability might be called popular or a leader. If his ability is exceptional, he is called a gifted musician or a gifted ballplayer. We seem to understand these terms and their connotations and, in the broad sense of the word, these individuals are all gifted. But some confusion arises when we want to distinguish between exceptional intellectual ability and these other gifts.

We should refer to someone with unusual intellectual ability as a gifted thinker or as intellectually gifted. But in practice, we do not. When parents or educators speak of a child who is gifted, it is commonly understood that they are referring to **a child with superior mental ability:** the one we used to call "really smart." This child is the one about whom this book is written.

HOW BRIGHT IS BRIGHT?

There is no magical line separating the superior from the average, but we seem to keep looking for one. For some reason we (society) seem to be more comfortable when we can put people, other people, into categories. "She's a socialite." "He's a radical." "Oh, you teenagers!" When we use these terms, we assume we have evoked a total picture of the person described, but we really haven't. The confusion results from varying interpretations of such words.

This compulsion to fit people into categories has caused us to look for more and more exact ways to distinguish those who are gifted from those who aren't. Although there is a need to define the term, we must realize that each definition of intellectual giftedness will reflect the particular use for which it is intended. A psychometrician, a scholar, an educator, and a parent might use differing terms, or interpretations of terms, when describing the same child. Also, over the years, because of our changing needs and developing ability to identify exceptionality, the definition of giftedness has been modified many times.

"Tenacious of memory and hard to deceive" was the description Plato used for his exceptionally bright students. For centuries this type of description sufficed, because we were satisfied that we could recognize a genius by his behavior, by the products of his efforts (he was the individual who would solve problems that most of us did not even know existed). But we humans, by nature inquisitive, refined our skills of observation and began to look more carefully at the most able among us, asking: "Just what is it that sets them apart? Could there be others who possess these same qualities, and how can we identify them?"

Tests were developed that could measure the degree to which anyone possessed some of the abilities observed in the brightest people. We began speaking of potential, of the ability to learn. As we became increasingly proficient at measuring mental prowess, it appeared that the illusive magical line had been found: The superior were those who scored in the top one or two percent on a specific intelligence test!

Success! Satisfaction—for a while anyway. Then, some of us began asking questions and detecting problems. It seemed obvious to J. P. Guilford, for one, that our ability to measure had far exceeded our understanding of what we were measuring. Guilford found that the intellect had many more facets than the tests were sampling, and he suggested that probably many others were yet to be identified.

Although IQ tests have been expanded and improved, their proponents contend that it is not necessary to test every factor to determine general intellectual ability. (More about intelligence testing in Chapter 12.) However, in the minds of many of those who must select certain children and provide for their special educational needs, **a discontent with the use of intelligence tests as the sole measure of giftedness remains.**

There is a trend, in the academic world, toward redefining giftedness to include a wider range of abilities than had been considered in the past. One of the new definitions, which is credited to Joseph Renzulli, looks at the interaction of three factors—above average ability, task commitment, and creativity—as they are brought to bear on a multitude of specific performance areas. In his view, giftedness does not exist in a vacuum. He suggests that the gifted are those who possess, or are capable of developing, this composite set of traits and applying them to any potentially valuable area of human performance.

We know that a child who can score in the top two percent thinks differently, at high cognitive levels, and has extraordinary educational requirements. Further, some children's talents have been uncovered by IQ tests whereas other methods have failed. However, educators admit that, for one reason or another, some gifted children are still left undiscovered.

If those in the academic world are having difficulty defining and detecting superior ability, where does that leave you, the parent? How can you tell if your preschooler is gifted?

IS YOUR CHILD GIFTED?

Many studies have shown that parents can be unusually successful in assessing their preschooler's ability. Parents have the advantage of being able to observe the child on a daily basis, under all sorts of conditions, over an extended period of time. They can usually spot giftedness by recognizing deviations from normal developmental timetables and having a picture in mind of what gifted children are like. (In Chapter 3 the characteristics of gifted children are listed and explained so you can be aware of them and perhaps be able to identify giftedness in your child early in life.)

The first thing you will probably notice in your infant is an unusual alertness; then you might become aware of his remarkable curiosity or a particularly long attention span. As the months pass, you are likely to be surprised at how much he seems to understand even though he has not yet begun to speak. He may begin talking early—though many gifted do not—and he will use language with unusual proficiency, expressing thoughts early and employing rather advanced syntax. Later, as he gains command of the language, you will be amazed by the amount of information he has absorbed so early and how quickly he seems to "get" things. **If you see these qualities in your preschooler, you can be pretty sure yours is a gifted child.**

When speaking of preschoolers, we are naturally referring to potential, as we know that many aspects of giftedness will not manifest themselves until later in life after the emergence of other abilities, skills, and interests. The great artist must first learn to hold a brush; the writer must learn the rules of grammar; the home run hitter, to hold a bat. The degree to which this potential is inborn or attributable to the manner in which the child is reared is more closely examined later in this book. But from the outset you should know that **parents must be aware of the tremendous effect their perceptions of a child's potential, from as early as the moment of birth, have on the ultimate emergence and character of ability.**

Psychologists are now considering the possibility that certain characteristics and abilities we have long assumed to be inborn might be the result of, or have been influenced by, an unaware parental conditioning from birth. (Although recent studies concern various gender-related characteristics, the findings might be applicable to differences in mental ability.) For example, some studies show that new parents treat boy infants differently from girls. It has been observed that they view their new babies quite differently and very predictably according to their sex. Boys are handled more roughly, spoken to less softly, seen as larger, stronger, and more alert than girl infants. Such typical parental behavior is manifested throughout the child's life—from the kinds of chores he is asked to perform to the games he is encouraged to play. It is being suggested that these ways of treating boys differently from girls, rather than any inborn differences, may be the cause of the many dissimilarities we note between adult male and female individuals. The significance to you, the parent, is to recognize the likelihood that your perception of your infant's capacity is one of the factors instrumental in the development of his capacity. There could be more than just a modicum of truth in the old saying that children are what they are expected to be.

THE CRITICAL YEARS

The first few years in the life of your gifted child and his experiences during this relatively short period have a critical impact on the kind of adult he will become. This is the time when the foundations—for good or bad—of all physical, social, emotional, and intellectual development are being laid. Regardless of the kind or the amount of potential with which your newborn was genetically endowed, the ultimate fulfillment of his promise is directly related to the quality of his early environment and the development of crucial perceptions, attitudes, and personality traits.

The manner in which an individual perceives himself and views the world plays a major role in the extent to which he is able to benefit from any educational opportunities. His perceptions are determined largely by the caliber of parenting he receives from the earliest days of his life. As a person matures, his perceptions color all his experiences and affect not only the quality but also the quantity of knowledge he can draw from life. Two people can have what to all appearances are identical experiences, yet, because of the way each perceives what is happening, the results can be quite dissimilar. This phenomenon explains why an artist, a naturalist, and a hunter will return from a walk in the woods with very different impressions of what they saw on their outing and why one adolescent might view parental authority as oppressive, another as just or benevolent.

You may have observed that if you are interested in a particular topic, or have some previous knowledge of it, you will "get" so much more from a lecture by an expert in that field. Or, when you learn a new word—one you are sure you have never heard before—all of a sudden you realize it is being used over and over in reading materials and conversations. Your previous experiences and attitude toward anything new cause you to see or not see things in your environment. Attitudes toward learning are formed early.

The time to think about cultivating your gifted child's receptiveness to good learning experiences is now, for the earlier the process is begun, the greater the chances for success. The importance of timing and ways to recognize the best time for encouraging certain abilities and attitudes are discussed later, but a general statement to keep in mind is that **the optimum time to nurture abilities is as they appear,** and the time to decide what to nurture is before the fact whenever possible.

The more parents of a gifted child understand about the needs of their offspring as a developing human being and as an individual with special needs commensurate with his exceptional ability, the more likely they will be able to provide the proper nurturing environment. We recognize that much of what is applicable to the rearing of a gifted child can apply to all children, and vice versa, and we are convinced that, given a stimulating, caring environment, all children could be more gifted.

PARENTING THE GIFTED: DEVELOPING THEIR POTENTIAL

The acquisition of knowledge is actually one of the least important factors affecting the development of a child's cognitive, or mental, ability and the use to which he will put this ability. **It is the self-concept he forms as a result of his relationships within the family, as well as the values and attitudes he acquires in the crucial preschool years, that greatly determine the extent of the fulfillment of any potential with which he was "gifted" by nature.** The development of abilities involves important individual behavior patterns—such as the way one approaches problems, reacts to frustration, and relates to other people—that have become so firmly established by the fifth or sixth year that they are difficult to moderate and, in some cases, impossible to change in later life.

Parents aware of their enormous influence on the total development of a child and cognizant of how quickly this developmental explosion takes place will be more inclined to expend the time and energy needed to provide a healthy nurturing environment for their child. A parent armed with the knowledge of developmental patterns and gifted characteristics will be more able to recognize and appreciate early signs of giftedness for what they are.

Parenting a gifted child is not easy; it is an important task with long-lasting implications. There are rewards—now and in the future—for helping your youngster develop his potential, but you must be willing to pay the price. There will be days when it will take more time than you have; it will tax your energies and test your capacity to cope with frustrations and doubt. You will have to make countless decisions, learn to trust your judgment, and overcome preconceived notions about where, when, and how learning takes place.

In the past, many of us were programmed to believe that anything related to learning is best left to the schools, that teachers are the experts and therefore parents have no business entering into that domain. We are all becoming increasingly aware, however, of the phenomenal amount of learning that takes place in the preschool years and are starting to realize that to deny a child certain experiences simply because he has not reached school age can be counter-productive. For example, gifted children typically demonstrate an early interest in the so-called academic subjects such as reading and writing, math, and science. The parent who feels free to encourage other interests might be reluctant to approach these subjects with the same confident enthusiasm. But these are a part of the gifted child's life and they demand immediate attention rather than being deferred to that arbitrarily predetermined "learning" period beginning with his entrance into school.

Many of us assume, simply because reading traditionally is taught to six-year-old youngsters in the first grade, that this time and atmosphere are the best for all children to learn to read. It is further assumed that the schools know the best way to teach such "academic" subjects. (Incidentally, the best way is the one that works and may be different for different children.) Even when we sense instinctively that our children are interested and could learn many of these things earlier in the home, we might fear "pushing" them or increasing the chances that they will be bored when they do enter school. Later chapters examine the distinction between pushing and encouragement, the fact that most things are best learned when the desire to learn them first appears, how to combat classroom boredom, and some of the many things that can best be learned in the home.

Certain societal pressures can also cause problems for parents of gifted preschoolers. Sometimes society views the intellectually precocious child as a freak and the parent of that child as misguided. Have you noticed that it is acceptable to admit you have a vision of rearing a future president, but not another Einstein? We hear artistic parents asked if their child inherited an artistic talent, but we would never dream of asking an intellectual if his child was smart. This is simply not done!

Society seems willing to make special provisions for the development of many talents and abilities, but cries of "elitism" are sounded when considerations are made for the intellectually precocious. The child and his parents can be made to feel embarrassed by his gifts; some even go to great lengths to hide them. A healthy attitude on your part would be to accept that your child's giftedness is as much a part of him as his brown eyes or long legs. Just as you know you will have to adjust the length of his Levis for a proper fit, so you will need to adjust his environment to fit his cognitive ability. Neither fact should be a cause for bragging or complaining. These are simply the realities of life.

We are accustomed to the typical picture of Dad out practicing football with his little O. J. Simpson or Joe Montana, or yelling instructions and encouragement during a Little League ball game. We see mothers running themselves ragged, sacrificing time and money to get their little Baryshnikovs or Dorothy Hamills to ballet or skating lessons.

We accept these parental actions as normal and caring. But what would our reaction be to the following scenes?

> Dad, at the office water cooler, bragging about his five-year-old who has just finished writing a lovely poem.
>
> Mom rushing Sally to logic lessons with Professor Steinmetz at the local university.
>
> Instead of packing up for a weekend at the beach, or a trip to see a tennis match, the family is excitedly planning an overnight trip to visit a library in a nearby city.
>
> A preschooler being allowed to join in an adult conversation and even being encouraged to contribute his thoughts.

The first set of examples (the Little League father and the backstage mother) are fictitious yet typical. The latter are neither fictitious nor typical. They are actual incidents related by parents who were asked to recall examples of behaviors that earned them disapproval or were questioned as unwise. (We would certainly not want to make judgments concerning the value or appropriateness of any of these activities without knowing more about the circumstances—such as the interests and ability of the child and his parents.) The point is that **gifted children do have needs and interests that are not typical or normal, and their parents are sometimes criticized for the manner in which they meet these needs.** If you find that having a child who is different causes you to feel alone or if you need help in coping with often-distressing societal pressures, Chapter 5 lists numerous sources of valuable assistance.

As the parent of a gifted child you will find that you are playing in a different ball game than many of your contemporaries. Somewhere along the way it will become apparent that your child is somehow unusual and has abilities, needs, and problems that are unique and must be dealt with in a unique manner. By the same token, you too are special—an individual who also happens to be a parent. Perhaps the only thing you have in common with other parents is the fact that you have a child. Since parents come in all sizes and shapes, with all kinds of attitudes and interests, with varying degrees of expertise, there can be no ideal mold or pattern for a perfect one. But there are some characteristics of successful parenting worth noting.

A good parent will be caring and informed. All of us make mistakes and misinterpret clues and so will you, no matter how much you know about giftedness and child development or how sensitive you are to the clues your child gives as to his needs. In a caring atmosphere, these little mistakes are not so important. When you respond to your infant's crying, you might not know just what the cry means—it might be that he is hungry, but you change his diapers. The fact that you are responding is what really counts. Your baby is learning the basics of communication. It will not be long before he learns to give out more appropriate clues to get the response he wants. More importantly he is learning that you care; this helps him build the foundations of a good self-concept.

As to just how much information a parent must have, we might consider what William Shockley meant when he spoke of "the principle of least knowledge." Some people, he observed, spend so much time learning everything there is to know, that they end up doing nothing. It is the wise parent who is possessed of enough of the basic knowledge to know the correct questions to ask, as well as how to obtain needed answers.

While no single source can possibly impart all the available information about gifted preschoolers—nor is it necessary for any one parent to be all-knowing—this handbook provides an overview of the essentials and tells you where to find additional information you may need. (Suggested readings and many helpful organizations are listed in Chapter 5.) And it gives particular attention to various parenting techniques or options, how children learn, normal behavior for the gifted, the fundamentals of development, and ways to nourish abilities and deal with the negative influences that have been found to stifle them. The book's primary message is that **the essentials of successful parenting include a reasonable degree of knowledge backed up with a large dose of common sense, together with the realization that the emotional climate in the home is far more important than specific child-rearing techniques.**

PARENTAL RESPONSIBILITY

Why do we advocate special treatment for gifted preschoolers? For the same reasons we would want any child to have his particular needs met. The child who differs substantially from others requires help adjusting to these differences so they do not become handicaps impeding the development of a whole, self-confident, productive personality. Numerous studies show that needs are best met as they emerge, and **many of those needs unique to the gifted child are best met by the parents and the family in the early years of life.**

The significance of the parent's role in the intellectual development of a child has been recognized in many cultures for centuries. The ancient Chinese had a proverb: "One parent is worth a thousand teachers." **Parents create the environment within which all kinds of learning—positive and negative—takes place.** Parent-child interactions that usually take place in the home have the greatest and most lasting impact of all life's experiences on the future of a child.

The parent of a gifted child has, in addition to those responsibilities common to all parents, a particular responsibility to recognize exceptional ability as it emerges and to provide an environment in which it can flower. **As exceptional abilities appear, the parental role takes on added dimensions, one of the most critical of which is decision-making.** You must decide what is best for your child, And wise decisions will be based on certain criteria:

- Acceptance of the fact that your child is an individual who just happens to be gifted. (His needs are many and varied, involving more than just his mental capacity.)

- Knowledge of your own and your child's unique abilities, interests, and resources.

- Identification of values, skills, and behavior you want to nourish. (You must begin early, as those traits essential to a productive life are grounded in the first few years.)

- Awareness of various parenting techniques or options.

- Basic understanding of how children learn and the factors that affect learning.

- Familiarity with normal developmental patterns—social, emotional, intellectual, and physical.

- Recognition that gifted children's behavior is often different from that of their peers.

- **Acceptance of the fact that you are only a partner with your child.** (In the long run, you may not accept all the credit—or in some cases blame—for his accomplishments and behaviors.)

As a parent with a knowledge of the characteristics of the gifted and the factors that affect their development, you will be more understanding of your child's behavior. You will be more likely to provide appropriate reactions, to recognize behavior that may need professional attention. You might be more tolerant when you realize that it is your preschooler's curiosity that is driving him to take apart everything he can lay his hands on or to ask countless questions—some of which you either cannot or do not want to answer. How you react to such behavior can spell the difference between over-indulgence and repression.

The farmers have a saying: "Give a pig and a child everything they want, and you will have a fine pig and a rotten child." **Your child needs your guidance and your wisdom.** (Don't be afraid because he may be smarter than you; you have age and experience on your side.) A child who cannot control himself, who is inconsiderate or just plain spoiled, will have a hard time in life no matter how bright he is.

But parents must also be careful lest they unwittingly repress the very qualities they want to encourage. While you certainly cannot nourish abilities that do not exist, some make their appearance and, because they are ignored or quashed, they go away.

Is a neat room really more important than a child learning to persist at a project or to concentrate on something so hard that time seems to be forgotten? These are the kinds of questions you will have to answer daily when living with a gifted child. Perhaps, as with many things, the ideal approach may lie somewhere between the extremes. A neat room is certainly important, but there are times when disorder is an integral part of "something happening." Maybe the room can be straightened **between** projects, or a certain space could be set aside for his work.

You will soon find that you can make reasonable compromises with your child, and he with you. You will be amazed at how reasonable the gifted child can be when you **explain things and lay down clear guidelines.** There are times when some rules may be relaxed, and your child is capable of learning to judge which ones these are and when overstepping them is allowable. **Teach him and trust him.**

With the highly gifted child, the sky may be the limit, but in order to fly sky-high he must first learn to use his wings gradually. You should expect a lot of him, but your expectations must be tempered with the knowledge that he can have developmental limitations as well as great ability. There will be times when you find yourself consumed with pride in his accomplishments; this is a natural feeling. But you must remember your basic values, be proud of the important things. Is it kindness, honesty, or industriousness that you want to encourage in your child; or do you value more material gains, or fame, or power? Your child will sense your priorities. Remember that most of the things he learns, he will learn by example and personal experience. You cannot force a child to be kind; he learns kindness by experiencing it himself. Show him. While there are no guarantees that he will learn and practice the things you teach and value, the odds are certainly with you.

You might have all sorts of preconceived notions and expectations as a parent. One of them could be that you really expect your child to share all your interests. Even if he doesn't, you will be shortchanging him if you don't expose him to those things you enjoy. He might not take to the books you like or the music you delight in; his idea of a good time may differ from yours. He may not want to follow in **anyone's** footsteps, but he can "catch" your enthusiasm and learn to appreciate others' preferences, just as you will learn to appreciate his.

You **can** expect your gifted child to do more and do it sooner than the books about child-rearing would indicate. You will probably have to let him try his wings sooner. But if you have planned for that day and have given him roots and helped him gradually develop a good sense of self-worth, of independence, and of responsibility, you will be ready and so will he. In the final analysis, as Mark Twain once said, there are only two things of real lasting value we as parents can give our children:

Roots and Wings.

2

The Great Debate

Are some people smarter than others because of superior genes, or is it the environment that causes the difference? The question continues to arise and many of the answers continue to confuse. Just as we become comfortable, accepting the evidence from one point of view, the opposing side renews its efforts to get us to listen to its convincing arguments.

There have always been individual differences in ability, but since the development of systematic measures of these differences—we call these measures IQ tests—we have been forced to consider **hard** evidence the "experts" present to distinguish the bright from the less-bright. Genetic scientists have learned more and more about inherited factors that play an influential role in all areas of human development, including the intellectual. Social scientists record differences among groups of individuals, which they believe can be attributed to cultural conditions. The differences psychologists, educators, and parents see in children, are presented in case studies that apparently provide the proof necessary to support their competing theories.

Who are we to believe? There would be no problem if we could just listen to the spokesman with the best credentials, but highly qualified experts hold conflicting views. We could disregard obviously biased viewpoints; but even if we do, there still remains a large body of clearly impartial evidence to be considered. The authorities cannot seem to settle the question once and for all. This is a controversy that simply will not go away.

WHY DOES THE DEBATE CONTINUE?

An unresolved question always holds a certain fascination. When we recognize similarities and differences among people, our natural inclination, being curious and inquisitive, is to ask "why" and to search for an answer. We buy the books that present evidence for or against the genetic factor; we turn on the talk shows and read the popular magazine articles telling us of new studies claiming to offer the solution.

There is, however, a reason more important than mere curiosity to continue looking into the causes of intellectual superiority or deficiency. Research into such matters could find the cures for severe disorders, help individuals develop more fully, and increase the general level of ability and productiveness of the whole human race. Geneticists have given us the tools to detect the probable occurrence of various genetic defects and the means to avoid many of the common forms of mental retardation. Proponents of environmental influence are pushing us to provide a more stimulating atmosphere for our children from the earliest days of their lives. The schools are being forced to rethink their positions about the kinds of situations into which students are being placed.

We must be careful not to ignore or reject particular research findings on the nature/nurture debate because of personal biases or because the topic, today, can often involve controversial questions of basic differences among the races.

We must also learn not to read implications into statistical evidence too early, or try to apply generalizations to individuals. We must recognize that evidence seeming to point out differences between groups may not be applied indiscriminately to individuals within that group, for it is well known that **no matter how people are grouped, the differences among the individual members of that group are usually greater than the differences between the groups.**

The resolution to the debate will continue to elude us if we are looking for an either/or answer. The answer will undoubtedly be expressed as a matter of degree of influence. **No one would say that intelligence is 100 percent inherited or that it is fully caused by the environment.**

THE SWINGING PENDULUM

To put the whole nature/nurture question into perspective, it would be helpful to look at some highlights in the history of the debate. The search for the answer has taken many forms over the years. The earliest observers simply noted differences and accepted them. It was a long time before anyone began wondering if something other than innate ability accounted for these differences.

One of the first recorded studies began in 1799. In that year, a young medical man in France took on a project that was to have lasting implications and would give us much information about the nature of intelligence.

Jean-Marc-Gaspard Itard was the physician to a new institute for deaf-mutes when he heard of a wild boy discovered living in the woods near Aveyron, apparently abandoned and forced to survive in isolation. Itard, an ingenious teacher and scientist, was granted permission to attempt to "humanize" the child. He kept detailed records of his work.

Itard concluded that physical and intellectual development are simultaneous and reciprocal and that the child's animal-like behavior was caused by lack of interaction with other humans. Initial success, then the limitations he later faced, led Itard to realize that not only is timing important, but that **without early significant socializing experiences, the mind and the senses will not develop.**

In 1859, Charles Darwin, a giant in the field of observation of other species of life, published his **Origin of Species.** Darwin's theory gave the proponents of the heritability of intelligence a scientific basis on which to build their arguments. For years thereafter people generally accepted the "fact" that intelligence was inherited.

Partially as a consequence of Darwin's evolutionary doctrines, the scientific community began more intensive study of individual differences between human beings. The search was on for a measure of those differences. The belief, at this time, was that everything came to us through our senses: Good senses were equated with good intellect. Hence, measurements of sensory thresholds were produced.

Then, in the early 1900s, psychometricians began developing psychological tests to measure the differences the scientists had been observing. The intelligence test was born.

The first IQ tests sought to measure a single entity: intelligence. Later, numbers of specific abilities were isolated and measured separately. As these abilities were examined, it became apparent that their development was influenced by experience and learning. The pendulum of opinion in the nature/nurture debate was beginning to move toward the experiential side, impelled by the findings of two of the most important experts on human behavior.

Sigmund Freud and Ivan Pavlov, working separately and using quite dissimilar techniques, introduced evidence that much of human behavior was affected by life's experiences. During the 1920s it was popularly accepted that the experiences of the first few years determined future intelligence.

Less than ten years later, a pediatrician, Arnold Gesell, began his detailed observations of the effects of the environment, or culture, on the development of children. His theories were to have an enormous and lasting impact on the general thought about the genetics of the intellect, educational policy in the schools, and approaches to parenting. Gesell found that all children advanced physically, intellectually, and socially in regular, predictable stages. **The culture, Gesell said, helps the child to achieve his developmental potentialities, but the process is always limited by the child's natural** (internal) growth process—maturation. Gesell was not impressed with the power of early experiences to influence development.

For some time the belief that there was a biological basis for intellectual differences prevailed. This attitude was helped, in part, by Jean Piaget's theories of intellectual development, which were gaining in popularity in the 1930s and 40s. Piaget, a noted Swiss psychologist, described stages of cognitive development through which each child passes on the way to maturity. He believed it was not possible to speed up the process by adjusting the environment. Most parents and educators alike were convinced that children grow and learn naturally; what and how much is learned is determined by a combination of heredity and maturation. A strong "hands-off" philosophy pervaded early-child-rearing practices in the United States.

Then a social revolution and a scientific shock were to give the next nudge to the pendulum. With the civil rights movement, born in the 1950s, the thought that intelligence was determined by the genes became generally repugnant. Educators began searching for new techniques to develop the intellectual capacity of all students, and parents were given advice on how to increase the intelligence of their offspring. The federal government initiated programs, such as Head Start, to compensate some children for their lack of a stimulating early environment.

The Russians' launching of Sputnik not only sent shock waves through the scientific community, it jolted the educational establishment into a flurry of activity. The Space Race was on and we were all to be participants in one way or another.

The National Academy of Sciences held a conference to consider the nature of the learning process. The spokesman for this group, Jerome Bruner, expressed the belief that **anyone can be taught anything, provided it is presented in a suitable manner.** Another influential voice heard during this post-Sputnik period was that of Benjamin Bloom, who attributed the differences in general intelligence to the environment **and to the amount of encouragement a child receives.**

Educators took another look at Piaget's stages of intellectual growth and Maria Montessori's "sensitive periods" for learning and interpreted them to mean that the difference between good intellectual development and poor was determined by timing and the quality of the environment children are exposed to during the early stages of their lives. Maturationist theory got into the backseat with the theories of heritability.

We have become comfortable and secure in our conviction that what we do as parents and educators—the environment we provide for our children—does make the difference. That is, until we turn on the latest TV talk shows, pick up current popular magazines, read the books on the best-seller list. We are detecting a trend back to the belief in the heritability of intelligence. Some geneticists are pursuing the concept that certain humans are born with a predisposition to intellectuality, much as some are born with a predisposition to specific diseases. And neuroscientists are finding correlations between the normal spurts in brain growth and periods of intense learning in children. Names such as Shockley and Jensen, and terms such as sociobiology and DNA are in the popular vocabulary and bantered about in discussions (arguments) about the relative importance of genes and the environment.

WHICH IS IT?

The best position to take in this debate might be that **no matter how strong the genetic factor, intelligence does not develop in a vacuum without interaction with the environment.** Heredity probably sets the potential for growth, but **it is the rare individual who reaches his upper limits.**

Intellect is not like blue eyes or brown hair. Many, many factors (both genetic and experiential) contribute to a complex trait such as intelligence, and these variables certainly interact in complicated ways. **Intellect is responsive to the environment.** If a child has innate capacities for intellectual tasks, he needs a stimulating environment to develop them.

We can only speculate on which of the differences in intellectual functioning are caused by the environment and which by genetics—most experts will admit to at least 20 percent influence on either side. **Heredity sets the limits and is relevant to intelligence, but the correlations are low, suggesting the decisive role of experience.**

The environmental input begins from at least conception: maternal nutrition, the baby's need for oxygen to the brain, illness during pregnancy. In addition, since all human experiences go through various cultural and personal filters (we call this perception), it is difficult to predict with any accuracy the total effect of any one experience. "The same fire that melts butter, hardens steel."

WHAT DOES THIS MEAN TO YOU?

Perhaps the outcome of the nature/nurture debate does not really make any difference to a parent who realizes his child is gifted. To a certain extent, the parent provides the child with **both** the genes **and** the nurturing environment.

There is not much you can do to change your child's heredity now, but you can affect the climate in which he grows. If he has the potential to be six-foot-three, you would not restrict his food and exercise to keep him under five-five. Nor would you deny him the chance to develop his mental potential. If he has the vocal chords of a Luciano Pavarotti or the backhand of a Tracy Austin, you would certainly provide the kind of environment in which his special talent could grow. But, more importantly, you would be aware that there is more to becoming great in any field—more than a natural ability and appropriate opportunity.

Perhaps the range in abilities and/or mental capacities is really less than many suppose. Is is currently being suggested by persons observing the lives of the greats of our society that **there is something in addition to heredity and environment related to the development of any special ability**—something that comes from within the individual. It has furthermore been suggested that **this inner drive, or achievement personality, has, to a large degree, its roots in the first few years of life.**

Wise parents, realizing that their child's heredity is already set, will learn about how intelligence and personality develop during the critical first few years. They will then **set the environment in the home (and the relationships within the family) to increase their child's chances for developing whatever potential he has.**

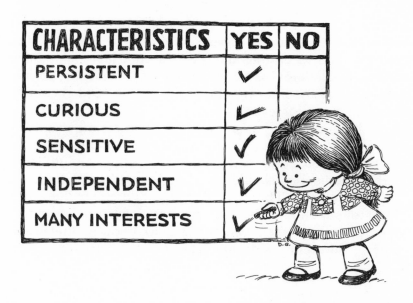

CHARACTERISTICS	YES	NO
PERSISTENT	✓	
CURIOUS	✓	
SENSITIVE	✓	
INDEPENDENT	✓	
MANY INTERESTS	✓	

3

What Are the Gifted Like?

Gifted children **are** different from their age peers and the more highly gifted they are, the more pronounced these differences become. The gifted seem to possess, in a greater degree than the general population, certain distinguishing traits, or characteristics. The purpose in listing them is to give you, the parent, some clues for identifying uniqueness in your child and some idea of what typical behavior to expect. This should allow you to recognize those qualities you value, and want to encourage, and those you might want to temper or discourage.

The characteristics listed here are those commonly used by parents and other observers to describe gifted children in general. While it is helpful for a parent to become aware of these distinguishing attributes, it is just as important to understand that **all gifted children are not alike.** They come in a variety of packages and differ from each other in a myriad of ways.

Some of these traits appear quite early and are often the first clue the parent has that his is an unusual child. Others may appear later as skills (such as speech, reasoning, reading, and the like) are developed. Some need encouragement to grow, or even to remain. Some you will want to nourish deliberately; others will not seem so important. The presence of some might make the difference between a productive, gifted adult and one who is either unfulfilled or perhaps indistinguishable from the general population.

The parents who know what gifted children are like will be more tolerant and understanding in their personal day-to-day interactions with their own gifted child, knowing that, **sometimes, "different" is normal and not necessarily bad.**

CHARACTERISTICS OF THE GIFTED

One of the most common observations about gifted children is that they seem to possess **insatiable curiosity.** They are often described as "excited about everything under the sun," as wanting to know the causes and reasons for everything, with an inner urge to explore their world. They ask countless questions (frequently provocative ones) and demand answers (usually not the routine ones). They try to understand complicated things and seem to be more interested in "how" and "why" than simply "what."

Exceptional persistence and an **unusual power of concentration** are often noticed early by the parents of gifted preschoolers. These children commonly become so interested in doing something that they do not want to stop. They possess the ability to involve themselves totally in a problem area for an extended period, refusing to be distracted. They seem to have a need to devour a subject and, not easily discouraged by failure, they are willing to spend extra time on things that interest them.

The gifted are noted for their **wide range of interests.** Rarely bored, they always seem occupied. These youngsters know about many things of which their peers are totally unaware. They exhibit an early interest in encyclopedias and atlases, in events and problems about which other children have no concern. They have many hobbies and are more interested in new activities than in the "same old thing."

Some gifted children begin talking very early, but many begin relatively late, seeming to wait until they are ready to speak in complete sentences. It is not when they start; it is, rather, their **use of language** that distinguishes the gifted ones. They delight in conversation, using language to communicate: to share feelings and information. The very young use grown-up words correctly and whole sentences early. They use language to explain things, often going into great detail about how something works or why they did something. Books, written language, hold a special fascination for them.

A **remarkable memory** characterizes many gifted children. They tend to retain what they have seen, or heard, or read, resulting in a large store of unusual facts and extensive information about many things.

They **willingly accept responsibility** and are remarkably reliable, trustworthy, and conscientious. Apparently aware of their ability, they can usually be counted on to do what they say they can do—and do it well.

An **independent individual,** the gifted child prefers to be on his own, to be self-sufficient, to care and do for himself. Many of his pursuits tend toward solitary activities; and while he might be described as a loner, he does enjoy people—usually older children or adults. He is not satisfied with the simple or obvious; his thinking could be described as independent too.

Seeking order and consistency in the world, the gifted child **likes to organize and bring structure to people, things, and situations;** yet, at the same time, he accepts disorder caused by details. More than noticing details, he has an extraordinary sense of which ones merit his attention. When he collects things, he also organizes and classifies them. He has a special capacity for planning, organizing, and seeing relationships, which is often apparent in his desire to organize groups of his peers. He can see common elements in situations, deducing generalizing principles, and usually shows an early interest in consistent things such as clocks, calendars, and numbers.

This child **catches on quickly and easily** and is impatient and bored with routine tasks. He finds lack of progress frustrating. While some gifted children are described as slow, this slowness can usually be attributed to caution, the desire to be thorough, great interest, meticulousness, or simply the desire to think things over.

His **leadership ability** (sometimes viewed as bossiness) stems from his tendency to dominate and organize, his sociability, and his enthusiasm. He generally directs the activities in which he is involved; he is able to figure out what is wrong with an activity and can show others how to do it better.

The gifted child see **humor** in situations where others may miss it. He has a quick wit and gets the point of jokes. He loves "I wonder what if . . . ?" games. This sense of humor develops early; parents often see it as a special insight by which these children can detect the incongruities in their surroundings.

The **ability to grasp abstract concepts** and see abstract relationships is evidence of giftedness. This child is greatly interested in cause and effect, in the difference between reality and fantasy, in performing difficult mental tasks. He can reason things out. He is possessed of an unusual degree of foresight, thinking ahead to possible results that other children (and adults) miss.

A **sensitive** person, the gifted child responds emotionally to stories and the needs of others. He is thoughtful, understanding, aware, and interested in adult problems (divorce, death, war); he often seems driven by a desire to be of service and can be unusually considerate of the feelings of others.

The gifted can be characterized as **critical of self and others.** Dedicated to perfection, they are generally intolerant of stupidity and dissatisfied with their own accomplishments. They have little tolerance for gray, being interested in absolutes: right and wrong, good and bad.

They are **alert and perceptive** with keen powers of observation, often seeing things others miss. They seem to be more aware of what is going on around them.

Their **creative problem-solving ability** is apparent. They are full of new ideas, imaginative, resourceful, and inventive, often suggesting better ways to do things. They have a capacity for identifying and clarifying problems, getting to the heart of situations, and seeing the flaws in things. Rather than being frustrated by problems or difficulties, they are challenged by them.

Energetic, versatile, and experts in self-initiated learning, they seem to be **self-motivated**. They have the ability to look ahead to distant goals, putting off rewards. They are flexible and often excel in everything they do.

As you read these descriptions of the gifted, you can form in your mind a fairly accurate picture of what a group of gifted children would be like. However, it is most important to remember that if you were to take each child separately, you would undoubtedly find that some of them do not possess all the characteristics listed here, nor do they possess these qualities to the same degree.

One other point should be made clear. There is some question if all of these traits are actually a function of giftedness or if they are more descriptive of children of a particular cultural or socioeconomic background, or of those who are more easily identified as possessing those abilities we value in the cognitive domain. For example, one of the early studies of gifted children was conducted by Lewis Terman, who observed that they, as a group, were larger and healthier than other children (an observation that continues to be made in study after study, but which I deliberately chose to exclude from my list of descriptors). I do not believe these physical attributes signal giftedness. Instead, I suspect high ability is just more difficult to spot in the less-healthy child, or perhaps physical development is more closely related to nutrition, which in turn can be related to the cultural or economic background of the child. The relationship might be simply that it is awfully hard to be smart when you don't feel well.

PARENT CHECKLIST

Sometimes these charcteristics typical of the gifted are only apparent when we know what to look for, and often we don't realize our child qualifies until we add up the little clues. You could very well have a precocious preschooler in your family and still not be able to mark each item on the following checklist. As you now know, **not all gifted children have all the characteristics normally associated with giftedness.** If, on the other hand, you can go through this checklist and find that it rather consistently describes your child, then you have the clues and should consider the implications that he is either very bright or could be classified as gifted. **The difference between bright and gifted is only a matter of degree and the kind of nurturing the youngster receives in the preschool years is frequently the factor that tips the scale.**

DIRECTIONS: Check each item that best describes your child in comparison with other children at the same age.

AS AN INFANT:

_____ Noticeably alert and aware of what is going on around him/her.

_____ Displays unusual interest in new sights and sounds.

_____ Doesn't give up; works hard till he/she can do what he/she is trying to do.

_____ Responds to language in an appropriate manner, showing early signs of recognizing words such as "bottle," "Mommy," "bye-bye."

_____ Remembers familiar persons, places, or toys.

_____ Resists help; wants to do things by himself/herself (roll over, sit up, reach a toy).

_____ Seems to sleep less than other babies.

AS A TODDLER:

_____ Notices changes in his/her surroundings.

_____ Loves to explore; gets into everything.

_____ Spends extra time getting things right.

_____ Understands most of what is said around him/her.

_____ Remembers where things are.

_____ Wants to feed and dress himself/herself.

_____ Interested in how he/she can cause things to happen.

_____ Recognizes clues to your mood.

_____ Wants to be around people.

_____ Intrigued with books; will sit for long periods looking at pictures or listening to story.

_____ Always seems busy; looking, doing, touching, etc.

_____ Frustrated when kept in playpen, high chair, or such.

_____ Has a large vocabulary, adding new words so fast you can't count them.

AS A PRESCHOOLER:

_____ Wants to do things for himself/herself.

_____ Likes to try new things.

_____ Retains most of what he/she has seen or heard; remembers things you didn't even realize he/she knew.

_____ Likes grown-up things.

_____ Can anticipate the consequences of his/her actions.

_____ Seems to know just what he/she is capable of doing.

_____ Has a good sense of humor.

_____ Not easily distracted from the thing he/she is doing.

_____ Interested in all sorts of things.

_____ Uses and understands grown-up words.

_____ Can tell long, involved stories.

_____ Likes to figure things out for himself/herself.

_____ Catches on quickly and easily.

_____ Tends to dominate peer groups; influential.

_____ Versatile; does most things well.

_____ Likes consistent things (numbers, clocks, calendars).

_____ Quick to get the point of a joke or a story.

_____ Interested in relationships (grandmother to father).

_____ Sensitive to others' feelings; visibly touched by sad or happy stories.

_____ Likes to be with older children or adults.

_____ Is critical about his/her own work.

_____ Understands abstract ideas (time, death, good, distance).

_____ Can always find something to do.

_____ Can be reasoned with.

_____ Notices words on boxes and signs and asks what they are (maybe has even begun to read).

_____ Plays at writing.

_____ Is persistent; sticks to tasks that excite him/her.

_____ Can spend long periods of time in intense concentration.

_____ Loves to enlist adults in 2-way conversations.

_____ Assumes a protective or responsible role when around younger children.

_____ Can plan and carry out complicated activities.

_____ Is an expert at something; knows a lot about one thing.

_____ Is observant; notices things you miss, puts unusual detail in drawings.

_____ Shows imaginative use of toys and adapts common objects for inventive purposes.

_____ Full of good ideas and better ways to do things.

_____ Asks lots of questions and keeps asking until getting an answer that satisfies him/her.

_____ Sizes up situation before plunging in.

_____ Tries to understand complicated things.

_____ Wants to know how things work; asks reasons why.

_____ Not satisfied with routine, simple, or obvious solutions.

_____ Can wait for things to happen; has a sense of time.

_____ Is able to manipulate situations to get what he/she wants.

ONE IN A MILLION

While we can delineate a rather comprehensive image of gifted children in general, there is, at the very top of this group, a minuscule percentage of individuals differing as greatly from other gifted youngsters as the typical gifted child differs from the average. I am speaking of ability that is so rare it occurs statistically only once in a million—the genius.

The chart below* will give you some idea of how rare the incidence of genius is:

APPROXIMATE IQ	EXPECTED NUMBER OF CHILDREN
130	3 out of 100
150	1 out of 1,000
160	1 out of 10,000
170	1 out of 100,000
180	1 out of 1,000,000

The child who tests at 180 IQ is as extreme, intellectually, as the most severely retarded is on the other end of the spectrum. This observation is what causes some educators to label these one-in-a-million children as the "severely gifted."

The figures in the chart are statistical figures, representing the number of gifted children you can reasonably expect to find in the normal population. That is, you might expect to find one gifted child in an average classroom, one with a IQ above 150 in a junior high school, and only one above 180 IQ in a large city or small state. You must realize that **these numbers will not apply to every group of one hundred, one thousand, or one million children.** There may be no IQs above 130 in one group of one hundred children, and 6 in another; but the average would be three. Moreover, for

*Adapted from R. A. Martinson and L. M. Lessinger, "Problems in the Identification of Intellectually Gifted," **Teaching Gifted Students,** ed. J. J. Gallagher (Boston: Allyn & Bacon, Inc., 1965), p. 27.

various reasons (including cultural advantages, employment opportunities, educational facilities) **the gifted tend to cluster** in some regions more than others.

Can you imagine how it must feel to be **that** different from one's peers? The severely gifted must learn a painful lesson: other human beings are inherently different from them.

Who are these people, the geniuses among us? We cannot be sure, but most experts include in their lists such names as Voltaire, Isaac Newton, Auguste Comte, Francis Galton, and Michelangelo.

What do we actually know about the extremely gifted? Not really very much, there are so few of them.

One source of information about genius is biographical. Norbert Weiner, whom we know for his theory of cybernetics, recounted personal incidents in his own childhood, telling of how he was raised by parents who firmly believed that he should take time to play as well as time for work. He emphasized the fact that although geniuses are often quite normal in many aspects of their lives, this normality frequently causes them problems of acceptance by adults. For example, some of us will not allow a four-year-old who speaks like an adult the luxury of acting like a child. Weiner, who had a superior grasp of mathematics, was exceptionally late in being able to master multiplication—even to the extent that he had to count on his fingers to get the answers. His teachers had trouble accepting this anomaly common in prodigies.

Another source of information about the extremely gifted is a comprehensive study, directed by Leta Hollingworth, involving a group of children with IQs above 180. Hollingworth found that the really difficult problems of adjustment to life and people come to those at the extreme end of the intellectual spectrum (180 to 200 IQ). Such a child needs an enormous amount of love and understanding from his family to be able to cope with the problems caused by his superior ability. Hollingworth's findings prompted her to define the "optimum intelligence" as between 125 and 150 IQ—the range most favorable to a successful, well-rounded personality in today's world. Fortunately, this is the range within which most gifted children fall.

NOTABLE ACHIEVERS

You might ask: "What about the Darwins, the Brontës, the Lincolns? Where on the scale of intellectual diversity would a Mendelssohn fall?"

Catherine Cox tried to find the answers to just those questions. She studied the writings of a group of persons notable for their unusual achievements (there is a critical difference between high ability and unique ability) and used these writings to make an estimate of the probable IQs. Cox recorded two scores for each person: one was an estimate obtained from writings produced before age 17; the other from writings generated between 17 and 26. Look at some of her estimates and notice how many of them fall within the range Leta Hollingworth described as optimum.

	AGES: 0–17	17–26
Charlotte Brontë	155	155
Humphry Davy	150	175
Charles Darwin	135	140
Michael Faraday	105	150
Abraham Lincoln	125	140
Henry W. Longfellow	150	160
Felix Mendelssohn	150	155
Thomas Macaulay	180	165
John Milton	145	170
Issac Newton	130	170
William Pitt, the Younger	160	180
George Sand	150	173
Voltaire	170	180
James Watt	140	145

You might have noticed that not only are there discrepancies (in some cases quite large) between the two scores given most of these individuals, but the estimate on Newton seems rather low. What we can learn from this table, however, are three important facts:

1. Estimates of ability can be in error.
2. It does not take a genius IQ for significant accomplishments.
3. An IQ score is not a stable entity.

NURTURING THE WHOLE CHILD

From all the sources of information on the highly, and the not-so-highly, gifted, we have learned that most people of superior ability show it early. But in order for them to develop to capacity, they must be nurtured by more than the favorable conditions of encouragement, instruction, stimulation, and opportunity. This nurturing must be balanced with the satis-faction of basic human needs and the acquisition of social skills, because **intellectual ability is apt to run away with other phases of development.**

All children need companionship. The child who has little chance to interact with others runs the real risk of retarded social development. Undoubtedly, if there were some way we could find out, we would be appalled by the numbers of gifted persons who had "great" ideas or solutions to society's pressing problems but were unable to find a listener or a vehicle for their answers because they were unable to relate to others.

Because of the difficulty of finding playmates who share common interests, with whom they can communicate, the gifted sometimes retreat into solitary pursuits, fill the void with imaginary playmates, and/or gravitate toward older children and adults. Even when they are given the opportunity to interact with others their age, it soon becomes apparent that many differences exist.

Many of our future leaders can be expected to come from the ranks of the gifted. Leadership is an ability that often appears early and must be given the chance to develop, but the highly gifted, who have the potential for great leadership, are frequently inhibited from practicing these skills when they exclusively seek either solitary pursuits or older companionship during their formative years.

We all want our children to grow up with successful, well-rounded personalities, capable of fulfilling their own personal needs and meeting the challenges they will face in the future. We can guide them on their way by being knowledgeable and caring.

A knowledgeable parent can provide those elements needed for the manifestation of superior ability: encouragement, stimulation, instruction, and opportunity. **A caring parent will not ignore his child's basic human needs or neglect those additional needs unique to the child's giftedness.**

4

The Special Needs of Gifted Children

Your gifted preschooler shares common needs with all children, and the most basic of these needs is the security provided by **parental love and acceptance.** Without this, nothing else really matters much. If you can give your child unqualified love and can accept him for himself rather than for the prestige his accomplishments could bring, you will find that **he will be able to weather all sorts of parental mistakes you might make along the way.** Even normally debilitating circumstances (such as environmental deprivation or severe physical handicap, for example) seem to be tolerated much more easily by the youngster who is blessed with strong feelings of self-worth.

Sometimes, because they seem so mature and so self-sufficient, the gifted are denied the loving and petting other youngsters educe. This could easily be misinterpreted as personal rejection—and that could be devastating to a child who might already feel out of step because of his exceptionality.

High-level intelligence will certainly make demands on your child, demands that can cause undesirable behavior. If you are sensitive to changes in his behavior, you can frequently pick up clues to your child's needs. But sometimes the special needs of these children are not so apparent, nor are they reflected in their immediate behavior. Then how do you know what they are? You can only try to look into the future, anticipating the kinds of demands life will put on your gifted child and the skills he will need to cope.

Scott, for example, who will one day become a research biologist, must learn how to be organized, persistent, and attentive to details. Nancy, a future business leader, will have fewer obstacles to a successful career if she knows how to communicate effectively with her peers and if you teach her, now, to respect the accomplishments of those around her.

Your child's high potential for excellence can be enhanced or thwarted by the manner in which his special needs are met in his preschool years.

UNDERSTANDING

Are you able to react to your gifted child with understanding instead of criticism?

The primary need of a gifted child is parents who understand the special problems giftedness sometimes causes and who are able to help their child acquire the skills to deal with these problems as they arise.

Some of the very qualities we admire most in the gifted give them the most trouble. There is a fine line between personal attitudes society perceives as "good" and those considered "bad," and this line seems to float, depending upon who is doing the judging. At what point does persistence become stubbornness; confidence, arrogance; independence, rebellion; pride, conceit; open-mindedness, gullibility; sensitivity, vulnerability; curiosity, nosiness? When do we judge the versatile child to be spread too thin, and when is the specialist viewed as myopic? The gifted walk a tightrope and to step off brings criticism hard for a child to bear. You can react with understanding and help him see what is happening so he will be more able to deal with it.

Loneliness caused by being different, frustrations in school, and concerns they cannot share with their peers are all sources of potential grief for gifted children. You can prepare your child to face these realistically without trauma. If you really understand that your youngster is going to have to come to grips with the fact that he is not like everyone else, you can help him learn to cope with, and even value, being different from the norm.

You can see to it that "sameness" is not valued in your daily life. There is a great deal of pressure from the world to be "like the rest of us" and it would be very easy for the gifted to take that attitude.

Incredible as it may seem, in school, the one place the intellectual child should meet with success and receive positive "strokes," he often meets with just the opposite. The school experience can be terribly frustrating! Gifted students are often forced to spend most of their time waiting for the rest of the group to catch up. Many teachers feel threatened and react negatively when they think a child might know more than they do. In some classrooms there is really not much for the bright student to learn and the reward for being right is simply more to do.

The gifted are not allowed the luxury of just spilling out what they think; they must first consider the consequences. You can teach your child how to deal with this problem by sharing with him your similar experiences. Let him observe how you work things out—how you are willing to risk unpleasant personal consequences when you stand up for important causes—but also share with him your reasoning for letting some things go.

Some gifted children carry great burdens, worrying over matters they cannot talk to others about. They worry about life and death, about human relationships and personal development. They worry about injustices and farfetched repercussions. They even worry about family finances. **Some seem to**

carry the weight of the world on their shoulders. It helps to talk about things that bother us. Establish lines of communication early, then protect and nourish them; they are fragile.

An understanding parent realizes that an outstanding gift might be despised because it not only causes someone to be **so** different, but it also takes time away from other things. It can draw unwanted attention to a modest child. Helping your youngster handle such pressures requires a bit of sensitivity on your part: knowing what the problem is, how severe it is (or could be), and knowing just how much help to give.

Many gifted children, because of their advanced reading ability and language skills and because they absorb so much around them, pick up enormous amounts of surface information that frequently gives them the appearance of knowing more about a given subject than they really do. If you understand this, you won't make faulty assumptions based only on the things that come out of your preschooler's mouth. Imagine your five-year-old coming up to you and saying, "I know where babies come from, I read all about it in the encyclopedia." Can you relax now that he knows the facts of life? **Don't count on it.**

Finally, your gifted preschooler needs a parent who understands the role of curiosity in the development of the intellect, how strong this drive to find out can be, and how easily it can be squelched. Three-year-old Andre really wants to know "Why is Mr. Doe's nose so big and bumpy?" "What color is a heartbreak?" and "Why did Aunt Jane die?" You can try to answer. Or you can tell him to stop asking so many questions —in which case he surely will.

INDEPENDENCE

Do you give your gifted child opportunities to assert his independence?

All infants are born with the drive to be independent, but your gifted child is likely to retain this drive. Giftedness does not flourish in an atmosphere of dependence. While your child is certainly not ready at birth to "make do" on his own, it is not too early for you to start thinking ahead to the time when he will free of his dependence on you. You must be prepared to release him completely—and at an earlier age than you might expect.

Your infant will want to do things for himself from the beginning and this is the force behind most of his early learning. Your goal is to **promote the gradual development of his independence** by allowing him to be self-reliant. You can let him try things (within reason, of course) and if he needs your help certainly give it, but do not offer more than is absolutely necessary. Let him out of your sight (as his maturity will allow) by sending him on errands, letting him spend the night at a neighbor's or in a tent in the backyard. Teach him to dress himself as soon as he wants to learn and do not worry if the tee shirt is on backward or inside out.

Your independent thinker and doer will come up with some less-than-conforming behavior with which you will have to learn to be comfortable. At the same time, it is your responsibility to make it clear to him that there are times when he must temper his actions somewhat out of consideration for other people.

You can encourage him to assert his independence in his dealings with other people. Let him work out his relationships with his peers without interference from you. Let him explain to the toy store manager why he is returning the defective toy. Give him time to answer the questions adults (doctors, waitresses, Santa Claus) put to him.

By the time your gifted child reaches school age you should be in the background—there to jump in only when, and as far as, necessary. Do not do for him things he can do for himself.

Resist the temptation to smother your child with your attention. Respect his individuality, remembering that he is not an extension of your personality. If your child is secure in the knowledge that you love him and care what happens to him, he will thrive on this gift of independence. Let him go. Apron strings can strangle.

RESPONSIBILITY

Are you able to let your preschooler make choices and then live with the consequences?

Learning is a risky business and we must be willing to take risks, to try difficult things even when there is a chance for failure. We must be prepared to learn from our failures as well as from our successes.

The gifted youngster who never meets with failure will be at a disadvantage all his life. This is not to say that you should plan your child's life so he fails at everything he tries, nor should you go out of your way to provide him with an overabundance of success experiences. You only need to provide him with the environment in which he is free to make meaningful choices and is not sheltered from the consequences of his decisions.

Your attitude toward failure plays a part in building a positive attitude in your child. When your preschooler sees you ruin a new recipe by substituting oregano for parsley, he can learn a great deal from how you handle the situation. He can learn never to try to substitute one thing for another, or he could learn that one should not try to substitute oregano for parsley.

You can create situations in which your child can make choices and give him the skills to evaluate his own decisions. Give him responsibilities early, but be smart about the kinds you give him. Give him what he can handle and then trust him to be responsible. Even the youngest child can handle a certain amount of liberty. Let him have a part in choosing his jobs: ones he is interested in, sees as important, and can do well. **Then, get out of his way.** Respect his decisions even when they are offbeat or unusual. There is usually more than one way to do things. And you do not always have to tell him if he is right or wrong, especially if he can figure out how to correct his own mistakes.

Do not be tempted to overprotect your child. Encourage him to take risks, to try inventive solutions to **everyday problems.** If he fails, you can recognize his efforts and help him to learn to accept failure and frustration as part of learning and to profit from his mistakes. If, on the other hand, he succeeds, join with him in his joy of accomplishment.

You can prove to your little thinker that you value his decision-making ability by actually **using his ideas when you ask for them.** Remember also that the first step in solving a problem is the ability to see that a problem exists. The gifted have an uncanny way of seeing to the root of a difficulty, and this can be unsettling to some adults. Give him credit when credit is due. Listen to his ideas and judge them on their worth rather than on some other criterion, such as his age.

More and more, as your gifted child gets older, you will be allowing him do for himself what he says he can do—and he will usually be right! If sometimes his judgment is faulty, that will not be so terrible. If he has learned all along to deal with failure, if he is not afraid to get himself into something in which failure is a possibility, if he is secure in his ability to evaluate his own decisions, then he will be getting something good out of all different kinds of situations.

MODELS

Do you surround your child with the kinds of people you would like him to emulate?

Children model themselves on the people around them. You are your child's first, most continuous, and most influential model—so, **be the kind of person you want your child to be.**

It is obvious that children tend to talk the way their parents do, eat, walk, and dress as they do; but it may not be so obvious that their way of dealing with other people is modeled on the manner in which their parents acted toward them.

Your child will absorb all sorts of attitudes and behaviors from his early and constant contact with you (or whoever is his primary caretaker). How you communicate is manifest in the way you answer the telephone, speak to the sales clerk, converse with your mother-in-law. How you cope with stress is all too apparent to a preschooler (though sometimes a child this young is not able to understand the cause of your stress). Your child is exposed to the way you handle your car in a traffic jam, the way you cope when the roast is burned, and how you react to a broken glass. Your child can see the tangible results of doing without something in order to get something more important in the future; or he will learn that his parents expect immediate rewards and are not willing to work together toward some distant goal.

Even a four-year-old can learn to make value judgements by watching his parents on a shopping trip, choosing a new home, or deciding which political candidate to support. Your offspring are not going to be your clones, but much of the way they approach life will be modeled after you or the person with whom they spend the bulk of their time.

As your child grows, his circle of acquaintances grows and they all play a role in his development. Toward the end of the preschool years, it will suddenly become evident to you that your child is seeking adult models outside your home. Into conversations will creep bits of wisdom he has garnered from the butterfly collector in the next apartment, a neighborhood retiree who loves to talk about the old days, the blind lady who sits on her porch and "sees" so much, the gardener down the block. You will be amazed; you did not even realize that Mr. Jones collected butterflies, or that Ms. Smith knew where the new interstate was going through.

Your gifted youngster might need some help from you in meeting some other adult models: an artist whose success and joy in life comes from persistence and hard work; a humanitarian who is able to fulfill herself through devotion to the needs of others; a business man who must use his acumen, his willingness to take a risk, along with his thrift, to make a go of his concern; a scientist who must sometimes forego even basics like food and sleep to attain his goal; a scholar whose love of books and learning is a contagious joy.

Maybe you do not have an Edison in your neighborhood, or a Maya Angelou. You probably do not know a Margaret Mead or a Churchill, but you can introduce your child to these and other wonderful characters; you and your child can get to know them intimately, through books. You can learn of, and talk about, their successes and their failures, of the way they were able to use or overcome personal handicaps, of the happiness or tragedy in their lives.

Eventually, some gifted children, particularly the highly gifted, need to come in contact with other highly gifted people (peers and adults) to learn ways of dealing with the special problems of extreme giftedness. This need is particularly acute in the adolescent years, when nature gives all children a yearning to be part of the pack. The highly gifted youngster needs assurance that he is not alone in his differentness, that others like him have coped, that it is "okay" to feel terribly alone and frustrated. To see someone else coping, to be able to speak to someone who has had the same feelings, helps. To know that someone else understands and cares, makes it bearable. This period of adolescence can be a source of great frustration to a parent who has, until this time, been able to be all the resource his child has needed. But you cannot do it forever. It is just the nature of the beast for a youth to look for models outside the home. All you can do is be supportive and perhaps help him find the models he craves.

LIMITS AND GUIDANCE

Do you take the time to see that your child understands there are certain limits to behavior? Are your attempts at discipline directed toward the development of his self-discipline?

You will not be doing yourself or your child a favor by letting him do whatever he wants, whenever he wants to. In today's world, **all of us must accept some limits set by others.** That is the way our society works.

Because they can see injustices in some of the conventions we may accept, the gifted become impatient with, and sometimes rebel against, rules. Because they can find better ways to get things done, they view some rules as unnecessary. It is also true that the gifted, by virtue of their cunning, are frequently able to "get away with" things. But the fact is, the person who tries to function completely outside the limits of society will be met with frustration all the way.

Help your child understand the importance of living with others' limits. Giftedness is no excuse for offensive behavior. Set reasonable limits within your own family, set them early, and expect compliance with them. Be wise about the kinds of limits you set; there is a great difference between authoritive and authoritarian limits.

The early development of an internal locus of control is enormously important for your gifted child: his ability to get along with others, and even the probability that he will ever be able to get things accomplished, are often tied to the amount of self-control he has. He will need self-control to develop his good ideas beyond the nebulous stage. When he enters school, he will find that most of his learning will depend upon his ability to push himself to do things on his own. If he has become used to you pushing and nagging him to complete projects, he will expect the same from the teacher.

Gifted youngsters enthusiastically express their ideas and their reactions to other people's ideas in such a way that others sometimes feel intimidated by what they view as negative traits: critical, argumentative, domineering, and the like. The child who learns to control this enthusiasm in certain situations that might threaten others will have fewer social problems, and at some stages in life—particularly during the later school years—this takes on greater significance.

The enthusiastic student can also earn the wrath of the teacher when he anticipates answers and solutions, then lets the cat out of the bag prematurely. With a little self-control, this student can learn to allow the other students to experience the thrill of discovering things for themselves as the teacher had planned.

How do children learn self-control? The foundation is laid in the cradle and will be as strong as the baby's sense of trust. The infant learns to delay gratification when he finds his needs will be met. He will tend to develop inner control if he perceives from the earliest experiences that his environment is something he can manage. If, on the other hand, he learns early that he cannot take charge of the things that affect him, if he comes to expect someone else always to be there to order his world for him, he will not develop self-control.

Although some of us have difficulty accepting the fact, the gifted need guidance in many areas of living. **No child should be left to grow like a weed!** Some very well-meaning parents, wary of pressuring their child, do just the opposite—providing neither pressure nor guidance.

The gifted often succeed at so many things and have so many projects they want to attack, they sometimes need help confining themselves to a reasonable number of undertakings. Most of them need guidance in selecting worthwhile projects on which to expend their considerable energies. Yet, it is a parent this child needs, not a drill sergeant.

All children should be expected to live up to a reasonable standard of behavior. The gifted must additionally learn to assert their independence and to express their sensitivity and their empathy without antagonizing other people. They must learn to recognize how much nonconformity is acceptable while, at the same time, learning to judge those circumstances in which conformity is inappropriate.

Be interested in your child's interests. Encourage him to finish what he has started, but do not demand it. After all, he may have gotten all there is out of what he was doing, and some things (let's face it) are just not worth finishing. Teach him to know the difference.

There is a time to offer a helping hand and a time to get out of the way. There are times when your advice is needed and there will be many more times, as your child grows older, when you will not feel equipped to give it. This is especially true of vocational alternatives. If he has learned to respect the opinions of other people, to use them as the valuable resources they are, he will be likely to be successful in his search for the guidance he needs. If he has learned to filter what he hears through his own personal standards, interests, and abilities, he will take the advice if it is good, and ignore it if it is bad.

SOCIAL SKILLS

Are you willing to go out of your way to see that your child has the opportunity to develop his social skills in a variety of situations?

Some of the most serious problems that a number of gifted young adults face (depression, dropping out, hostility, self-destruction) can be related to their inability to form satisfactory personal relationships. Your child must be helped to understand and accept the fact that **he might not have as many friends as his peers seem to have and he might have to search longer to find compatible companions.** But he cannot wait until he is in his teens to discover this.

Everyone needs a friend and sometimes the gifted need help locating one. Most little girls and boys have a special buddy with whom they can share life's special secrets. Your gifted child might miss out on this important relationship if he cannot find someone of his own age with whom he can communicate.

When the gifted child has trouble finding an intellectual peer of his own age, he looks to older children or even adults for the companionship he seeks. This is normal and natural, but these older friends may not be able to share those silly little experiences that are such an enjoyable part of growing up. Knowing this, you might want to look around for other bright youngsters and arrange for them to meet your child.

While the observation of researchers—that the typical gifted child is popular—is generally true, most gifted children desire something more. They seek deeper relationships and are likely to be dissatisfied with casual friendships.

In your efforts to expose your child to socializing activities, you should take care not to push him through an overscheduling of his activities. And do not try to convince him that everyone else has scores of friends. This just is not so. Few children (or adults) have many friends of the kind your gifted child is probably looking for. One best friend is usually enough.

The friendship patterns of gifted children differ from those of other children. It is not at all unusual for a gifted child to have one friends for every interest: a fishing buddy, a music buff, someone with whom to work on a scientific problem, a chess mate, and a running partner. A person's age seems to make very little difference when the gifted choose their friends, although many of them seem to be a bit more comfortable in a slightly older group. The gifted actually have two sets of peers: those of the same age and those who are their intellectual equals.

The gifted need a chance to develop social skills, and socializing opportunities should be presented to the them early. They grow up so quickly they sometimes miss learning how to get along with other people. Sometimes, too, their cognitive development has been emphasized to the neglect of the whole child. Try to insure that your child's first socializing experiences are positive ones—starting in your home and then gradually increasing the number and frequency of outside contacts.

Your child needs a chance to socialize with people of various talents and abilities so he can learn to appreciate their individual contributions. Exposure to human shortcomings can help him accept both his own and those of others. He needs opportunities to work, as well as play, with other children so he can learn how things get accomplished through cooperative efforts. He may also learn to be assertive without being hostile or aggressive and to speak his mind without being domineering. All this will be possible only if he has gained a certain self-confidence—the self-confidence that is born in successful, early socializing experiences.

TO BE HEARD

Do you really listen to what your child has to say?

"If you know it, show it." I saw a poster carrying this message in the office of the guidance counselor in a school for the gifted. Could it be that superior students must be enjoined not to hide their talents? How could this happen?

Part of the answer may lie in the homes of these youngsters. Gifted children have so many ideas and are so verbal, that it is a temptation for adults to tune them out. They ask so many questions, it is easy to ignore the ones that seem insignificant.

Another reason may be that, since it is hard for them to find age peers who care to talk about the same things and in the same way as they, these verbal children have learned to choose the more-limited subjects others are interested in. The intellectually superior enjoy playing with words and ideas and using friends as sounding boards. If they are frustrated in their search for a sparring partner, they may stop verbalizing.

Because gifted children usually have a wide range of interests and can converse intelligently on many subjects, there is a tendency for parents to think these verbal children really know more than they actually do. The best way to avoid this trap is to listen carefully to what your child is saying and be ready to correct any misunderstanding he has.

You will be doing a great deal of listening over the next few years, for your child will have much to say and you should want him to feel free to do so. You can contribute to his good mental health by training him to talk to you about his feelings. When you **really** listen, he learns that how he feels is important to you. You will have opened up avenues of communication which will serve both of you well in the coming years.

A SUPPORTIVE FAMILY

Can your child always count on the family members for support?

Your child does not grow up in a vacuum. He is part of a family and the quality of the interpersonal relationships within the family are critical to his development.

Gifted children are in particular need of a support system they can count on without any reservation. These children can be their own worst enemies—they are so critical of themselves and their accomplishments. A supportive family will help your child recognize his own strengths and accept his weaknesses in a realistic light.

How can you insure that your home will be a source of support for all the family members? You can see that each member, adult or child, can express his feelings and thoughts freely without fear of rejection. Honest praise and encouragement should be offered for successes, and problems worked through in a positive rather than a critical atmosphere.

When your child moves outside his home he will, no doubt, meet some people who will do all in their power to downplay his successes and emphasize his failures. A supportive background is going to help him cope with this social phenomenon. He knows his shortcomings; he does not need others pointing them out. His family helps him accept the fact that we all have limitations.

Do not let him blow either his ability or his limitations out of proportion. If he cannot be made to feel comfortable within his own family, what chance do you think he will have of finding his place out in the world? Let him know **it is okay to be smart**—just as it is all right to make mistakes.

Your family must sometimes tolerate, or even approve of, behavior that seems inappropriate at ages four or five, but with the gifted we must often throw away any preconceived ideas that smack of age norms. You may be able to avoid some later sibling conflicts by using a criterion other than age for determining when something may or may not be done. For instance, one child might be allowed to cross the street at four years old and another not until eight. Your decision may be based on the specific conditions at the time or the individual child's competence.

While competition between siblings may be inevitable, it ought to be minimized as much as possible so it will not interfere with family relationships. Here, your attitude may be the key. Security, support, and love must not be contingent on what each child does; **comparisons are seldom beneficial.** It is heartbreaking to hear a parent introduce the children in the family with labels attached to each name. "This is our bright Nancy, our pretty Sonja, our athletic Lisa, and our artistic Marie." This sort of attitude can be so limiting. The bright Nancy might also have artistic ability, but the implication in her parent's introduction is approval only of her intelligence. She is not expected to be artistic—and she probably will not be. In real life, **parents are seldom surprised by their children's accomplishments.** Each family member should be allowed to earn recognition in as many areas as possible, and one child's accomplishments should in no way detract from what a brother or a sister do.

A word about compliments. Although all children need approval along the way and appreciate compliments on a job well done or a considerate deed performed, you will find that the gifted grow to resent generalized or repetitive compliments. If your gifted youngster has painted a picture, you might not get the kind of reaction you might expect when you say, "My, that's a pretty seascape!" He is well aware of the faults in the painting. (The water may look muddy.) He can also see the good points. (The overall composition might be quite good.) So, compliment him on the composition. Be specific. Then, if he mentions the muddiness of the water, do not misinterpret this as ungraciousness. You can try instead to help him figure out what caused the muddy look.

GOALS

Do you let your children see you working toward worthwhile goals?

The people who seem to get the most done in life are those who set goals for their behavior and accomplishments. Your gifted child has the ability to do important things. **The level of his aspirations will determine the level of his accomplishments.** You will want to insure that your child expends his greatest energies on worthwhile undertakings. He can learn the joy of working toward, and ultimately reaching, goals by watching you do it.

You can expect your gifted child to have high aspirations. While you certainly would not want to discourage this pattern, you should realize that, at times, he may need help deciding which goals are reasonable for him. The gifted are often able to set incredibly long-range objectives and then direct all their energies toward achieving them. It is often astonishing to see what they can accomplish through their drive and persistence.

Goal focusing can help superior students get through some trying periods in the school years. When they can see a purpose in doing routine classwork—when it can be related in their minds to a specific goal—they will thereby fulfill a need they seem to have to see progress in what they are doing.

A few parents expect their children's goals to be the same as their own. You will only be disappointed if you do. But if you are content with your child's ability to set goals and work toward them, the chances are you will be happy with the kinds of goals he sets. There will be many times you will just have to get out of his way and trust him. He is not here to live out your unfulfilled aspirations; you can only try to raise a child who is one of those singular persons who aims high, and makes it.

VALUES

Are your values apparent to your child?

Because of his potential for influencing others, the gifted child needs to develop a strong value system against which he can evaluate the goals he sets, the choices he makes along the way. **Values give a direction to behavior that rises above all outside influence.** The independent child with superior ability must also learn to use his ability with discretion, developing early a sense of fairness and propriety.

While you cannot force your values on a child, they are made clear by the example you set. How you use your personal value system to direct your own behavior becomes all too apparent to those around you. To teach your child to be ruled by values rather than external rewards or punishments takes time. Discuss events relating to value choices, talk about why you will not support a certain candidate, tell him why you do not slide through a stop sign even though no one is watching. Let him see you give up some immediate satisfaction for something you think is more important. Tell him why you return to the store when the clerk accidently gives you too much change.

Keep discussions about values at a level he can understand. Encourage your child to openly express his feelings and opinions, even when they differ from yours. When he comes up with a good point, grant him that point.

A VARIETY OF MATERIALS

Do you select the materials in his environment with an eye to variety rather than quantity?

Your gifted child needs a stimulating environment, and the younger he is the greater the need for an interesting physical environment. The infant needs tangibles on which to focus his senses: things to touch and look at, to smell and hear and taste. While you are preparing your baby's environment, remember there is a difference between a good, stimulating environment and one that is overstimulating. If too many toys are supplied by an overzealous parent, they can distract a youngster rather than encourage him to direct his attention.

When you choose his crib toys, for example, you should look for things that might intrigue him. Look for toys with different textures, toys of various shapes and sizes, and colors. Select objects that react differently when they are hit: some that bounce back, or make a sound, or give resistance, or move out of reach.

As your child moves out of the crib into a widening world, he still needs variety. And do not be caught in the trap of thinking that everyting in his environment must relate specifically to his cognitive development. Choose things that he can have fun with, that help him develop physically and socially as well as intellectually.

The older your child becomes and the more aware you become of his unusual ability, the more your imagination and your knowledge of both child development and your own child's interests and ability is needed to select things that might capture or spark his interest.

You will find many of the things you choose for your gifted child might not be at all appropriate for other preschoolers. He will want to explore things and have interests beyond those expected of one his age. Do not let this bother you. And do not let the pressure you may receive from well-meaning friends and relatives bother you either. You know your child better than they.

Occasionally you will find that your gifted preschooler has become so involved in something that interests him that he almost totally ignores the new elements you place in his environment. Put the new books, or toys, or records away for a while. He will be ready for them shortly.

TIME

Are you aware that your gifted child has no more time in his day than anyone else has?

Overscheduling can become a problem for the gifted child, and parents and teachers are not the only villains. These children, who tend to have an excess of energy, who are interested in so many different things, who are capable of handling several projects at one time, are apt to take on more than they can handle. You can help by teaching your child to use some simple techniques for allocating his time.

You can see that your preschooler has some time alone— not to become a social isolate, but time to daydream, to think things over, to become totally absorbed in a task. At times he will be better off if he is just left alone, aware that you are there should he need you.

Parenting takes time, your time: time to stimulate, discuss, listen, interact, and guide. Be prepared to pay this price if you intend to be successful in this undertaking. Meeting your gifted preschooler's special needs will take a greater portion of your time than is demanded at any other period in your parenting experience, but it has the potential of being one of the most exciting experiences of your life. It can be fun. It can even be dull at times. But it will seldom be easy. There will undoubtedly be period of stress, as there are in all human relationships. Your gifted child will exhaust you, put excessive demands on you, try your patience, and cause you to ask, "Is it all worth it?"

Yes, it is.

5

You Are Not Alone

Just as the gifted child can experience the feeling of aloneness, so the parent can expect a sense of isolation stemming from an inability to find others who share common concerns. Your neighbor, who is worried because her six-year-old Johnny cannot read, is unlikely to lend a sympathetic ear to your fear that your four-year-old seems to prefer reading to socializing. Your co-worker, who will brag about her Little Leaguer's home runs, is not really interested in hearing of your little scientist's latest experiments. How can your sister-in-law empathize with your problems when Grandmother compares her average children unfavorably with your precocious child?

WHERE TO GET HELP

Sometimes all you need is someone to talk to—someone who will not misinterpret what you are saying. You might find it in a baby-sitter, the little lady down the street who raised a dozen beautiful kids, or the nursery school teacher.

Many parents of gifted children have found the kinds of help they need by consulting such sources as government agencies, gifted associations, books and other publications. Some of these sources are listed here for your convenience. Their purpose is to give help and support to parents like you. Use them.

GOVERNMENT AGENCIES

Federal Government: The U.S. Office of Gifted and Talented, is a division of the Department of Education. This office is a veritable clearing house of information and has a great deal of useful printed materials available for the asking. They even have a toll-free telephone number.

> U.S. Office of Gifted & Talented
> 6th & D Streets
> Donohoe Building
> Washington, D.C. 20202   ph: (800) 424-2861

State Government: Each state has either a Consultant for the Gifted or one person designated to disseminate information on the gifted. You can learn about all the gifted programs in your area by addressing your inquiries to the correct department.

> ALABAMA
>
> Consultant, Program for Exceptional Children and Youth
> 416 State Office Building
> Montgomery, Alabama 36130
>
> ALASKA
>
> State Department of Education
> Pouch F
> Alaska Office Building
> Juneau, Alaska 98801

ARIZONA

Consultant, Division of Special Education
Department of Education
1535 West Jefferson
Phoenix, Arizona 85007

ARKANSAS

Programs for Gifted/Talented
Department of Special Education
Arch Ford Education Building
Little Rock, Arkansas 72201

CALIFORNIA

Gifted and Talented Management Team
California State Department of Education
721 Capitol Mall
Sacramento, California 95814

COLORADO

Consultant, Development and Demonstration
Unit
Colorado State Department of Education
201 East Colfax
Denver, Colorado 80203

CONNECTICUT

Consultant, Gifted and Talented
State Department of Education
P. O. Box 2219
Hartford, Connecticut 06115

DELAWARE

Supervisor, Programs for Exceptional Children
Department of Public Instruction
The Townsend Building
Dover, Delaware 19901

DISTRICT OF COLUMBIA

Director, Division of Federal Programs
Office of State Administration
D.C. Public Schools
415 12th Street, N.W.
Washington, D.C. 20004

FLORIDA

Consultant, Gifted and Talented
State Department of Education
319 Knott Building
Tallahassee, Florida 32304

GEORGIA

Consultant, Programs for the Gifted
State Department of Education
State Office Building
Atlanta, Georgia 30334

HAWAII

Director of General Instruction
State Department of Education
1270 Queen Emma Street, Room 1206
Honolulu, Hawaii 96813

IDAHO

Consultant, Gifted and Talented
State Department of Education
Len B. Jordan Building
Boise, Idaho 83720

ILLINOIS

Coordinator, Gifted Program Unit
Office of the Superintendent of Public
Instruction
100 North First Street
Springfield, Illinois 62777

INDIANA

Division of Public Instruction
Indiana State Department of Education
120 West Market
Indianapolis, Indiana 46204

IOWA

Consultant, Department of Public Instruction
Grimes State Office Building
East 14th and Grand Avenue
Des Moines, Iowa 50319

KANSAS

Director, Programs for Gifted and Talented
and Creative
State Department of Education
120 East Tenth Street
Topeka, Kansas 66612

KENTUCKY

Coordinator, Gifted and Talented
1827 Capitol Plaza Tower
Frankfort, Kentucky 40601

LOUISIANA

Consultant, Gifted and Talented
State Department of Education
P. O. Box 44064
Baton Rouge, Louisiana 70804

MAINE

Gifted and Talented Department of Education
and Cultural Services
Augusta, Maine 04333

MARYLAND

Consultant, Gifted and Talented Program
Department of Education
P. O. Box 8717
Baltimore, Maryland 21240

MASSACHUSETTS

Division of Curriculum and Instruction
Department of Education
182 Tremont Street
Boston, Massachusetts 02111

MICHIGAN

Gifted and Talented
Michigan Department of Education
P. O. Box 30008
Lansing, Michigan 48909

MINNESOTA

Gifted Education Coordinator
State Department of Education
641 Capitol Square
St. Paul, Minnesota 55101

MISSISSIPPI

Division of Special Education
State Department of Education
P. O. Box 771
Jackson, Mississippi 39205

MISSOURI

Consultant, Gifted and Talented
Department of Elementary and Secondary
Education
P. O. Box 480
Jefferson City, Missouri 65101

MONTANA

Consultant, Fine Arts/Humanities
Office of Public Instruction
Helena, Montana 59601

NEBRASKA

Gifted and Talented
State Department of Education
233 South Tenth Street
Lincoln, Nebraska 68508

NEVADA

Consultant, Exceptional Pupil Education
Department of Education
Educational Services Division
Carson City, Nevada 89701

NEW HAMPSHIRE

Consultant, Department of Special Education
State Department of Education
105 Loudon Road
Concord, New Hampshire 03301

NEW JERSEY

Consultant, Gifted and Talented
State Department of Education
225 West State Street
Trenton, New Jersey 08625

NEW MEXICO

Director of Special Education
State Department of Education
Santa Fe, New Mexico 87503

NEW YORK

Supervisor, Education for the Gifted
320-A Main Building
Department of Education
Albany, New York 12224

NORTH CAROLINA

Coordinator, Gifted and Talented Section
Division for Exceptional Children
Department of Public Instruction
Education Building
Raleigh, North Carolina 27611

NORTH DAKOTA

Director, Special Education
State Department of Public Instruction
State Capitol
Bismark, North Dakota 58501

OHIO

Educational Consultant, Programs for Gifted
Department of Education
933 High Street
Worthington, Ohio 43085

OKLAHOMA

Coordinator, Gifted and Talented
State Department of Education
2500 North Lincoln Blvd.
Oklahoma City, Oklahoma 73105

OREGON

Coordinator, Special Education
State Department of Education
942 Lancaster Drive N.E.
Salem, Oregon 97310

PENNSYLVANIA

Gifted and Talented
Department of Education
P. O. Box 911
Harrisburg, Pennsylvania 17126

RHODE ISLAND

Consultant, Special Education
Roger Williams Building
22 Hayes Street
Providence, Rhode Island 02908

SOUTH CAROLINA

Coordinator for Programs for the Gifted and
Talented
Rutledge Building
Department of Education
Columbia, South Carolina 29201

SOUTH DAKOTA

Consultant, Gifted and Talented
Division of Elementary and Secondary
Education
New State Office Building
Pierre, South Dakota 57501

TENNESSEE

Consultant, Division of Special Education
State Department of Education
103 Cordell Hull Building
Nashville, Tennessee 37219

TEXAS

Program Director, Gifted and Talented
Texas Education Agency
201 East 11th Street
Austin, Texas 78701

UTAH

Consultant, Gifted and Talented
250 East 5th South
Salt Lake City, Utah 84111

VERMONT

Consultant, Special Education
State Department of Education
Montpelier, Vermont 05602

VIRGINIA

Director, Special Programs for the Gifted
State Department of Education
Richmond, Virginia 23216

WASHINGTON

Division of Curriculum and Instruction
Office of the Superintendent of Public
Instruction
Old Capitol Building
Olympia, Washington 98504

WEST VIRGINIA

Coordinator, Program Development
Division of Special Education
Capitol Complex
Charleston, West Virginia 25305

WISCONSIN

Consultant, Gifted and Talented
Department of Public Instruction
126 Langdon Street
Madison, Wisconsin 53720

WYOMING

Coordinator, Gifted and Talented
Department of Education
Hathaway Building West
Cheyenne, Wyoming 82001

GIFTED ORGANIZATIONS

There are many groups organized for the specific purpose of
helping the gifted child and/or his parent. They are aware of

the problems you and your child face and can offer not only support but expert advice.

Local Associations for the Gifted: These may be formed casually in the neighborhood and can be helpful as places to share experiences and through which to find other gifted children. These local organizations are often affiliated with state, regional, or national organizations. Ask the local school officials if one exists in your area. If none exist, you might consider forming one.

State Associations: Most states boast of one or more associations for parents and educators of gifted students. Your State Department of Education would be able to give you the name and address of the one closest to your area.

National Organizations:

American Association for the Gifted
15 Gramercy Park
New York, New York 10003

Association for Gifted & Talented Students
1627 Frankfort Street
New Orleans, Louisiana 70122

Association for the Gifted
Council for Exceptional Children
1920 Association Drive
Reston, Virginia 22091

Creative Education Foundation, Inc.
1300 Elmwood Avenue
Buffalo, New York 10422

Gifted Child Society
59 Glen Gray Road
Oakland, New Jersey 07436

Insight
821 Pennington Road
Elizabeth, New Jersey 07202

MENSA
1701 West Third Street
Brooklyn, New York 11223

National Association for Creative Children
and Adults
8080 Springvalley Drive
Cincinnati, Ohio 45236

National Association for Gifted Children
217 Gregory Drive
Hot Springs, Arkansas 71901

National Council for the Gifted
700 Prospect Avenue
West Orange, New Jersey 07052

National State Leadership Training Institute
on the Gifted and the Talented
316 West Second Street
Los Angeles, California 90012

BOOKS AND OTHER PUBLICATIONS

As close as your nearest library, or to be ordered from your
neighborhood bookstore, is a wealth of information. Listed
here are printed sources of material of particular interest to
parents of gifted children. The titles chosen elaborate on
subjects covered in this handbook, with the chapters to which
each entry relates listed in parentheses. Some are strongly
recommended for inclusion in your personal library; others
would be of interest for reference only or to the reader who
desires additional information on a given topic.

Books:

Baskin, B. H. and K. H. Harris. **Books for the Gifted Child.**
New York: R.R. Bowker Co., 1980. A list of books chosen
for their ability to challenge the imagination and talents of
gifted children. While it was compiled primarily for use by
the classroom teacher, it is a good source book for parents
and grandparents. See if your library has a copy.
(Chaps. 8,9)

Beck, Joan. **How to Raise a Brighter Child.** New York: Trident
Press, 1967. Although this book was written for all parents
(not just those with gifted children) there are many ideas
included that you can adapt to your own situation.
(Chaps. 1,6,7,8,9)

Bloom, Benjamin. **Taxonomy of Educational Objectives.** New York: David McKay, Co., 1956. Millions of teachers have studied Bloom's taxonomy, which details the ordering of the cognitive processes. While the book is long and its reading tedious, it is really worth checking a copy out of a nearby college library for skimming. (Chaps. 6,11)

Brown, R. and U. Bellugi. "The Child's Acquisition of Syntax," **Language and Learning: Investigations and Interpretations.** Cambridge, Mass.: Harvard Educational Review, 1972. This selection by Brown and Bellugi is a fascinating account of the development of sentences by the very young. For those interested in language, the entire collection of essays is recommended reading. (Chaps. 1,6,7)

Butler, D. and M. Clay. **Reading Begins at Home.** Auckland, New Zealand: Heinemann Educational Books, Inc., 1980. Informal ways parents can help build the foundation for their child's future learning. One chapter on direct reading instruction. This little soft-covered book, written by two teachers, is less than fifty pages, but it may answer some questions about how little children learn to read. (Ch. 8)

Cutts, N. E. and N. Moseley. **Bright Children: A Guide for Parents.** New York: G.P. Putnam's Sons, 1953. This is an old book, but you shouldn't have any trouble finding a copy in the public library. Although it does not address all the needs of today's parent, it nevertheless contains a good deal of basic information. Look for other titles by Cutts. (Chaps. 3,4,6,7,9)

Dennis, W. and M. W. Dennis, eds. **The Intellectually Gifted.** New York: Grune & Stratton, Inc., 1976. If you want to benefit from the collective views of the "experts" over the years, this is the reference book. Contains the works of Pressey, Gallagher, Hollingworth, Weiner, Terman, Cox, Galton, and others. Any teacher of the gifted ought to be familiar with these names. (Chaps. 2,3,6)

Fortuna, R. O. and B. O. Boston. **Testing the Gifted Child: An Interpretation in Lay Language.** Council for Exceptional Children, 1976. Contains good explanations of the language of testing. Describes the six major tests widely used to identify the gifted. (Ch. 12)

French, J. L. **Educating the Gifted.** New York: Holt, Reinhart & Winston, Inc., 1966. Good reference book for the parent or teacher of gifted school-age children.   (Chaps. 3,4,11)

Gallagher, J. J. **Research Trends and Needs in Educating the Gifted.** Washington, D.C.: U.S. Government Printing Office, 1964. One of the several volumes Gallagher has compiled of the research findings in the area of giftedness; all are of value to those who are interested in research. He also edited a textbook for teachers, **Teaching Gifted Students.** Boston: Allyn & Bacon, Inc., 1965.
(Chaps. 3,4,11)

Gesell, A. and F. L. Ilg. **Infant and Child in the Culture of Today.** New York: Harper & Brothers Publishers, 1943. Describes in meticulous detail the developmental stages from birth through age five. Extremely useful for detecting deviations. Parents report reading Gesell helped them understand and deal with the phases—good and not-so-good—that all children go through. Also listed are age-appropriate toys.   (Chaps. 1,2,6,7,9,10)

Ginsberg, G. and C. H. Harrison. **How to Help Your Gifted Child.** New York: Monarch Press, 1977. Written for parents of the school-age gifted child. Look for other titles by Gina Ginsberg if you have older children.   (Chaps. 3,11)

Guilford, J. P. **The Nature of Human Intelligence.** New York: McGraw-Hill Book Co., 1967. Guilford explains his "Structure of the Intellect Model." More on learning, creativity, child development (intellectual), tests, and the nature/nurture debate.   (Chaps. 2,6,12)

Hollingworth, L. **Gifted Children: Their Nature and Nurture.** New York: MacMillan, 1926. Leta Hollingworth is the expert on highly gifted children. If your child falls within this category, read anything you can find that she has written on the subject. You might be able to locate some of her books in a college library.   (Chaps. 2,3,6)

Itard, J.M.G. **The Wild Boy of Aveyron.** New York: Appleton-Century-Crofts, 1962. Itard's own account of his work with the young boy discovered wandering in the woods in Southern France. Fascinating.   (Ch. 2)

Jenkins, R.C.W. **A Resource Guide to Preschool and Primary Programs for the Gifted & Talented.** Creative Learning Press, 1980. Describes gifted programs all over the country for the young student. Lists identification procedures and instruments, personnel, and activities at different levels.
(Chaps. 10,11)

Lyman, H. B. **Test Scores and What They Mean.** Englewood Cliffs, New Jersey: Prentice-Hall, Inc., 1978. Comprehensive little book in which Lyman interprets test scores. You will need some background in statistics and testing to understand some of his explanations. (Ch. 12)

Montessori, M. **The Absorbent Mind.** New York: Dell Publishing Co., 1967. Maria Montessori expounds on the philosophy behind the schools that bear her name. You might not agree with all she says, but she writes well and convincingly. Worth selective reading. (Chaps. 6,7,9,10)

Passow, A. H. **The Gifted and Talented: Their Education and Development** (78th Yearbook). Chicago: University of Chicago Press, 1979. Wealth of updated information on the gifted. Scholarly style. (Chaps. 2,3,4,6,11)

Singer, D. G. and T. T. Revenson. **A Piaget Primer: How a Child Thinks.** New York: New American Library, Inc., 1978. Finally, someone has explained Piaget in terms we can all understand. Uses cartoons and exerpts from children's literature to make points. Includes discussion of Piaget's view of child's moral development. (Chaps. 6,12)

Spodek, B. and H. J. Walberg eds. **Early Childhood Education: Issues and Insights.** Berkeley, Ca: McCutchan Publishing Corp., 1977. The chapter "Understanding Infants" by J. R. Lally is worth the price of the book. Volume covers many issues of interest to those in the field of early childhood education. (Chaps. 1,6,7,10)

Torrance, E. P. **Dimensions of Early Learning: Creativity.** Sioux Falls, S. D.: Adapt Press, Inc., 1977. For those interested in the philosophy behind the Torrance Creativity Tests. (Chaps. 6,12)

White, B. L. **The First Three Years of Life.** Englewood Cliffs, N. J.: Prentice-Hall, Inc., 1975. White details the findings over the years at the Harvard Preschool Project. Heavy emphasis on the intellectual development during this critical period. If you have only one book in your preschool library, this should be the one.   (Chaps. 1,2,6,7,9,10)

Pamphlets:

Beautiful Junk* Ideas for creating free and inexpensive play equipment; suggestions for locating materials.   (Ch. 9)

Child Development in the Home* How to build self-confidence and self-discipline in the preschool child.   (Ch. 6)

Children's Choices Children's Book Council, 67 Irving Place, New York, NY, 10003. List of more than 100 books arranged alphabetically and by age level. Brief descriptions of favorite books; compiled annually. Free for 6½ × 9 self-addressed stamped envelope.   (Ch. 9)

Children and Television* How TV affects your life; how to help your child develop good television viewing habits.
          (Ch. 7)

Stimulating Baby's Senses* How to stimulate your baby's growth and development through the senses of sight, hearing, taste, and touch.   (Chaps. 6,7)

Teaching Your Child to Read* Games and activities to develop prereading skills.   (Ch. 8)

Magazines, Journals, Newsletters:

Gifted, Creative, Talented Magazine. G/C/T Publishing Co., Box 66654, Mobile, Alabama, 36606.

Journal of the Education of the Gifted. School of Education, University of Virginia, Charlottesville, Virginia, 22903. Quarterly Journal.

NAGC Newsletter. National Association for Gifted Children, 217 Gregory Drive, Hot Springs, Arkansas, 71901.

*These titles are all available from the Superintendent of Documents, Consumer Information Center, Pueblo, Colorado, 81009. Some titles are free; all are under one dollar.

National Network Director/Newsletter. Gifted Child Society, Inc., 59 Glen Gray Road, Oakland, New Jersey, 07436.

National/State Leadership Training Institute on the Gifted and Talented Bulletin. Attn: LTI Publications, Ventura County Superintendent of Schools, 535 East Main Street, Ventura, California 93009. 8pp.

Roeper Review. 2190 North Woodward, Bloomfield Hills, Michigan, 48013. Quarterly Journal.

The Gifted Child Quarterly. NAGC Headquarters, 217 Gregory Drive, Hot Springs, Arkansas, 71901. Quarterly Journal.

Talents & Gifts. 3912 Pembroke Avenue, Mobile, Alabama, 36608. Monthly Newsletter.

6

The Basics for Parents

A little learning is not always a dangerous thing. It is not necessary, or even possible, for parents to know everything about the broad topic of child development. However, if you want to encourage positive growth in your gifted preschooler, you really should have basic knowledge of what affects cognitive development and the fulfillment of potential.

GENERAL DEVELOPMENT

Age is not the best indicator of what to expect from children, especially the gifted. No child follows the "normal" rate of growth exactly, but **all children are subject to certain laws of development.** An understanding of these laws as they relate to the first few years is vital to effective parenting.

Some gifted children mature early, some do not. A few race through the developmental stages so fast, they appear to skip some of them. It is not at all unusual for a gifted child to be quite advanced in one area and slow in others — children are not confined to fixed developmental levels. While most development takes place in a predictable and orderly fashion, there is no reason to expect growth to be constant or smooth. Just as the organism seems to have spurts of growth and periods of rest in its physical development, so it may be in other areas of human growth.

PHYSICAL WELFARE

Studies of gifted children have revealed that, as a group, they tend to be healthier than other children. It has been suggested that the health and physical development of the gifted might be less a function of their giftedness than a factor that allows ability to emerge, but it seems reasonable to assume that it is really hard to be "smart" when one is not feeling well. Proceeding on the assumption that a healthy mind develops in a healthy body, parents will see that the physical well-being of their gifted child receives the proper attention.

Many good books on the physical development of children are readily available, so it will not be necessary to cover the subject here. You should have at least one comprehensive volume in your home for reference when you have questions about diet, childhood diseases, and the like. Ask your child's doctor to recommend a book.

SOCIAL DEVELOPMENT

It is fascinating to observe the infant evolve from a completely self-centered entity into a social being in just a few short years. A child is born aware only of himself—he is not even conscious that anyone or anything exists outside of himself. Yet, within a few weeks he has begun to sort things out, learning that he is separate and distinct from his surroundings.

His sense of self begins to form and develops in relation to the people around him. Its foundation is laid in the first few weeks of life. The infant who receives reliable love and attention learns to view himself as a worthwhile being. The infant's first socialization is with the person who meets his needs. As his cry is heeded, the seed of communication is sown; as his smile is returned and he is played with and enjoyed, his self-image begins to form.

By the middle of the first year he has become very sociable with his caretaker: he enjoys being talked to and played with. He recognizes strangers as such and is sometimes fearful of them.

Radical changes take place toward the end of the first year, when he begins to walk and move around in his world. He has, by this time, a good understanding of language and he suddenly becomes brave and starts to assert himself. Adults are looked to for approval and for assistance in situations he cannot handle himself. **How the people around him react at this time will have a great influence on his ability to interact with others later in life.**

Sometime before his second birthday the toddler seems to become fully aware of his independence; his world no longer revolves around his primary caretaker, to whom he expresses both affection and hostility. About this time, negativism erupts, often causing a "battle of wills" with his parents; but this negative attitude subsides, and his sociability increases.

True social interest in the outside world emerges around age three as the preschooler becomes more interested in playing with peers and less interested in home and mother. By this time the foundation of his personality has been laid and he will spend the next few years refining his social skills as he learns to view the world, not only from his own perspective, but as others do.

The rewards to the parents who facilitate their child's social development are great. The friendly, caring, secure, socially adept, gifted child is a delight to be around.

MORAL DEVELOPMENT

Your child learns right and wrong from you. Studies show moral development is fostered in the presence of parental warmth and love, in a home where the standards of behavior are reasonable, where transgressions rather than the child are disapproved, where discipline is appropriate, not unduly harsh or used to control.

To parents who believe they have done everything right, it can be very disconcerting, to realize that their preschooler seems to have no conception at all about right and wrong. It can be disconcerting, that is, to parents who do not understand that, just as language and bones develop from birth on, so children go through stages of moral development. Just as you understand why a three-year-old cannot run a marathon, so you should understand that **a preschooler deals with right and wrong in a manner that differs enormously from the way an adult would.**

Stages of moral development have been identified by both Jean Piaget and Lawrence Kohlberg. Piaget observed children of all ages and noted their attention to rules in their play; he also interviewed groups of students, asking their views about the rightness or wrongness of situations he would describe. A pattern emerged from which Piaget concluded that all children go through three distinct phases in their development: premoral (when the child does not feel bound by rules at all), conventional (when rules are seen as made by someone else, usually an adult, and are obeyed literally), and the final stage when the child's own moral principles rule his behavior.

Kohlberg's later research supported and expanded on that of Piaget. He found that four-year-olds, for example, would typically think of good and bad in terms of physical rewards and punishments ("The stove is bad to touch because it burned me."), whereas the six-year-old evaluates behavior in terms of labels ("Stealing is bad.").

Kohlberg specified six stages through which a person goes on the way to the highest level of moral behavior. During the first stage, the infant learns to do, or not to do, things because of the consequences (harmful things are bad; pleasant good). Later, that which fills a personal need is considered right (taking a cookie is okay because you are hungry). During the third stage, conformity rules behavior (what the group is doing is right and disapproval, like punishment, becomes something to be avoided). At the next level, law and order rule; then, those general rights agreed upon by society govern conduct. Finally, the most moral behavior, according to Kohlberg, is that which is dictated by the individual's conscience, which adheres to universal, self-chosen concepts or principles of justice. (Incidentally, not everyone reaches this highest level.)

Kohlberg said that persons do not entirely throw off the practices from the lesser levels when they reach a higher stage; rather, they gradually rely more and more on the higher motivations. He also found that mature conscience development requires a certain amount of cognitive maturation: the ability to go from concrete, rigid prohibitions to the more abstract, internalized standards.

All gifted children have an exceptional ability to listen to reason, to make use of what they learn, and to become self-directive. Talk to your child. Talking about his, and others', behavior can provide him with clues as to what is right and wrong, and gives him internal sources for evaluating his own behavior. **A high level of moral behavior is developed gradually, through stages, with parental help and guidance.**

LANGUAGE DEVELOPMENT

Perhaps the most exciting phase of your gifted child's development in the preschool years is his acquisition of language. The rate at which he increases his vocabulary is sometimes astounding; the manner in which he uses language, fascinating.

Language plays a fundamental role in the development of a child's intellectual and social skills. Once language begins, thought progresses: what he thinks and feels becomes clear when he learns to say it; the past can be remembered and the future anticipated through words. Precise communication becomes possible.

Language ability is more than the accumulation of words. Although in the beginning it is fun to count the words your youngster uses—in the beginning it is easy—it soon becomes an exercise in futility. The "average" one-year-old has a speaking vocabulary of three words; at one and a half, about 20 or 22. Most two-year-olds use 250 words, but some use fewer than a dozen and some have been known to have a vocabulary of over 1,400 words.

If, when your child is 18 months old, you can take an honest count of his vocabulary and find it is above 25, if he is quick to pick up new words and use them accurately, you can be sure he is bright. Yet, some very bright children do not talk until much later. An extreme deficiency does not in itself mean an intellectual deficiency or that he will have a language problem later. **The important thing to watch for in language development is understanding.** Your child should respond to simple commands by the time he is 10 months old. You need not be overly concerned about your two-year-old with a limited speaking vocabulary if he shows clearly that he understands what is being said to him.

Infants are born with the ability to hear and make all the sounds from which any language can be constructed. If English is the only language your baby hears, he soon loses his ability to hear and reproduce other sounds with ease. If he regularly hears English spoken with a Southern accent, he will speak with one.

In the beginning he can be heard amusing himself with the little sounds he makes and is soon reproducing some recognizable syllables. Sometime during the second half of the first year, your baby discovers that words are meant for him and he is on his way to the acquisition of meaningful language. A few months after saying his first word, he will probably be chattering all day, naming objects and occasionally adding qualities (big, good, hot). By three he will be using words in sentences as tools of thought; by four he will be asking endless series of questions; and by five he will be able to narrate long tales.

You can teach your infant new words by matching the sounds he already uses and by encouraging him to repeat them. You do this naturally and he delights in the game. But there is more to speaking than this type of mimicry; he must learn not only to make sense of words, but also the order in which words are spoken. It is incredible how readily the little speaker picks up the subtle differences in meaning expressed by the order of words. "Bye-bye, doggie" means something quite different from "Doggie bye-bye."

A child imitates and reduces sentences he hears. Some describe this kind of imitation as telegraphic English—the order is preserved but some things are just left out, much as we would do when composing a telegram. You might say to your baby, "Look, Laney, the doggie is running all over the yard." And Laney would respond, "Doggie run" or "Look doggie run." The order is the same and the meaning is retained; he just uses fewer words. Even though he may know hundreds of words there seems to be a limit to the number of words he will use in a sentence.

Parents naturally imitate and expand on what their children say. Your child will say a two-word sentence and, without thinking, you immediately come back with an expanded version of the same sentence, one that supplies the missing words and conveys the same message. Baby says, "Hot" and you return, "Yes, the soup is hot."

Language is a tool for communication and thought. The gifted child seems to have an early and lasting fascination with its use.

CURIOSITY

Nothing is more fundamental to a child's intellectual development than curiosity, yet we know so little about it. All children seem to come into this world equipped with an incredible amount of it. It is the motivating force that causes the infant to reach out, bat at his crib toys, drop things, replace hearing with listening and seeing with looking. What is it if not curiosity that makes a baby struggle so to learn to crawl, to get into things?

Why do some children enter school so full of curiosity, so eager to learn? Why is it others do not retain this high level of curiosity past infancy? Possibly the latter had their hands slapped too many times for touching interesting things or were told not to ask so many questions.

We know curiosity can be suppressed, but we also know we can encourage it just as easily. Act toward your child as if he is curious, recognize what excites him, prepare an interesting environment. Let him find out things for himself; let him get into things—within reason—and investigate his world; let him see you be curious.

The child who satisfies his curiosity does not stop being curious; quite the opposite, he seems to become even more curious about even more things. He apparently derives a great inner satisfaction from this kind of learning. The more he learns through satisfying his own curiosity, the more he seems driven to learn.

LEARNING

Knowledge of the general principles of learning can aid parents in providing an environment in which their child has the maximum opportunity to learn. However, it must be remembered that, like any theories, these may break down if applied absolutely to an individual. This precaution is particularly true with regard to the gifted, who not only think differently but often take inexplicable quantum leaps in their thinking processes.

When applying any theory of learning to your gifted preschooler, it is important to consider the real question: not how fast he can learn something, or how many facts he can learn, but how well the learning skills and attitudes he is building now will serve him in his future. You will want to offer stimulating and challenging experiences that can open up new vistas for your child to explore. You will be sure the experiences are appropriate to **his** level and interests, and offer help when it is needed.

Numerous theories have been advanced to explain how children learn, how they think, and how intelligence develops. While some may be oversimplifications that are not universally applicable, **theories are helpful in that they give us insight and direction.**

A few learning theories are described briefly here. If any one particularly makes sense to you, you might want to look into it further. However, in this matter there is safety in numbers. Skim through them all and let one modify another. (To avoid any implication of value or importance through placement, the theories have been arranged alphabetically.)

Behaviorism

Behaviorists define learning as a change in behavior. They deal only with observable behavior and operate under the belief that what is rewarded will be repeated. The behavior that is closest in time to the reward is the behavior reinforced. **As long as learning remains a pleasant experience, children will pursue it.** The behaviorists' approach seems to become less effective as the child matures.

Bloom's Taxonomy

Benjamin Bloom, and others, devised an ordering of the cognitive processes from the simplest and most basic (the acquisition of knowledge) to the highest and most complex (evaluation). Each level demands the skills and abilities of those lower in the order.

1. Knowledge—the basic material on which all subsequent intellectual operations are built.
2. Comprehension—a grasp of meaning.
3. Application—the ability to use appropriate generalizations or principles under differing conditons.
4. Analysis—the ability to identify parts, to detect how they are organized, to discover relationships.
5. Synthesis—creative work, the pulling together of elements to form a new whole.
6. Evaluation—making judgments using distinct criteria to determine the value of something.

Knowledge is basic to all learning but it is only the beginning: **Children should be encouraged to do something with the facts they know.** According to Bloom's hierarchy, before the learner can apply knowledge, he must first understand it. Creative work and good judgment, the two highest mental processes (levels at which the gifted operate much of the time) are possible only after the previous levels have been mastered.

Critical Period

Burton White, of the Harvard Preschool Project, is one of the experts who believe **the first few years of life are critical in the development of an individual,** especially in the areas of intellectual and attitudinal development. White narrows the critical period to that time between 8 and 24 months. Parents would do well to pay special attention to the selection of their child's primary caretaker during this short time span.

Developmentalists

The developmental, or stage, theories are most popular today. **They view intellectual growth as orderly and sequential.** Of the developmentalists, Jean Piaget, with his ideas on the stages of mental growth, is probably the best known.

Piaget saw the child as being in constant exchange with the environment—meeting its demands and making demands on it. He described the growth of the intellect in terms of a series of stages. During the first stage (birth to about age two) the infant deals with objects constituting his immediate environment. He has no understanding of the nature of classes or categories. During this stage the youngster eventually learns what Piaget calls the "constancy of objects": just because mother disappears from view, she is not gone.

The second stage (about two to six or seven) evolves out of the first. The child learns to use symbols and to think in terms of means and ends, but has difficulty with ideas like the concept of conservation: that the amount of water in a tall, thin container remains the same even when it is poured into a short, wide one.

Piaget divided each stage of intellectual growth into substages and devised specific tasks to determine at which level the child is operating. Some parents first learned of their child's giftedness when they discovered he could do some "Piagetian tasks" much earlier than other children.

Discovery Learning

Learning is something done by a learner, say the advocates of discovery learning, sometimes referred to as trial-

and-error learning; it is not something a teacher can hand to a child through communication. Admittedly, this kind of learning is time-consuming, but it becomes less so as the learner becomes more experienced. The infant in the crib must bat a ball time after time before he learns a batted ball can roll out of reach; a four-year-old may only have to make something happen two or three times to be able to generalize a rule.

Many times you will have to just sit back and let your child figure things out for himself. He must be willing to take many steps to find out what he doesn't know and this requires a certain amount of patience and persistence—but the result is an awareness that cannot be gleaned in any other way.

Inquiry

The inquiry method is similar to the discovery method in that the emphasis is on the child becoming an independent learner. **The focus of the inquiry method is on efficient learning by which the child becomes aware of the relationship between new events and that which he already knows.** The theory is that when a child is exposed to enough situations in which a principle is apparent, he will be able to use this information to predict outcomes of future happenings.

A child playing in the bathtub will discover that both his wooden block and a wood tongue depressor float. He might combine this information with the knowledge he already had, that a stick thrown into a pond floats, and come up with the generalization that wooden objects float. Since the goal of the inquiry approach is for the child to learn to formulate working theories, the premium is not always on being right. The learner is encouraged to test his theories and must be willing to accept that they may be flawed. When the child discovers a wooden object that does not float, he is encouraged to begin testing again and refine his theory to include his new observations.

Match Theory

Learning opportunities should match, or nearly match, the child's thought structure. **The child learns best when the task matches his stage of intellectual development:** the two-year-old is not going to get much from a lesson in perspective drawing, nor would most five-year-olds benefit much from instruction in how to crawl.

Piaget's "Optimal Mismatch Theory" is similar, but he advocated the presentation of tasks that are just slightly more difficult than those which the child can handle easily.

Montessori Method

Maria Montessori believed children have sensitive periods during which they are especially responsive to certain stimuli. **There are certain ages at which children learn some things more easily than at other ages:** it is easier to learn to walk at one year that at two months or sixteen years.

Montessori thought there was no need for direct instruction of the preschool child, **education being a natural process in which the child acts upon his environment.** Parents can structure an interesting environment that will stimulate the child and cause him to explore and learn.

Organizing Principle

A basic precept of learning is that as experiences become more complex there seems to be a need for some sort of organizing thread so learning will become lasting and transferable: **facts must be put into some kind of organization in the mind.** Jerome Bruner said, "The objective of learning is to save us from subsequent learning."

Sequence

There is a sequence to efficient learning: learning can be made easier when we **start with those things that are familiar and move on to the unfamiliar, or start with simple ideas before going on to the more complex.** Parents can help their gifted child get started on some difficult topic by introducing him to it in simple, familiar terms—and, if the child is interested in continuing, he can, with a minimum of parental assistance.

ofessionals were asked to rate the trait
ess in their field, creativity was found
ist. The creative scientist, lawyer,
comes up with many good ideas—is
ful one. Creativity is that which makes
a technician and an inventor, between
an artist. Performers who put their
creative skills to work on their art are the ones we remember
and admire. Most successful businesses were founded on the
good idea of a single individual.

But good ideas are obviously not enough—we all have
them but few of us would describe ourselves as creative. The
early signs of creative ability are visible in most young
children, in their play, in their approach to new stimuli, and in
their first attempts at expressing themselves through the arts.

Why aren't all of us creative adults? No one is really sure,
but many experts studying the question are now looking at
various factors in the early environment that might influence
the development of creative ability. The suggestion is that
creative thinking can be nourished.

As with other abilities, creativity manifests itself differently
in an adult creative production than it does in the early years.
But the seed is there and, if you know what to look for, you
will be better equipped to encourage the development of the
skills necessary for a creative child to become a creative
adult, the adult who has more than an occasional good idea.

Creativity in adulthood

Good ideas must be backed up with hard work if they are to
result in any significant productions and **creative productions do not simply happen.** They evolve out of a sequence of
stages, which can take minutes, hours, or even years. The
creative thinker is sensitive to problems: he sees imperfections that bother him and drive him in his search for a better
answer. He first begins scouting out information, gathering
pertinent facts, and calling on his personal store. He keeps on

probing until he is satisfied that he has all he needs before the serious work in his mind begins.

Then the subconscious begins working on various solutions; they are formulated and examined. It is a sort of incubation period for the creative thinker: a time of sustained individual thought that may require a period of solitude.

Sometimes a perfect solution comes immediately—like a flash. Frequently, though, the creative thinker leaves his problem temporarily to attack something else; all the while his subconscious is still working on the answer to the first problem. The creative thinker knows instinctively that there is a time to push and a time to wait. It is hard to be creative on schedule.

Then, seemingly without warning, inspired solutions seem to leap out like the hidden picture in a puzzle. Now, after what on the surface appeared to be a long period of inaction, the creative person begins working in a seeming frenzy—driven by some inner force. Solutions are tested, elaborated, and accepted or rejected (in which case the process begins anew).

Work on the creative production continues until the creator finishes it to his satisfaction. Then, for reasons unfathomable to an observer, the creator abandons his product—apparently uninterested in it anymore—and moves on to other matters.

When your gifted preschooler has a good idea, encourage him—but don't pressure him—to follow it through to completion. The youngster who sees that the cake you have just baked would look prettier if he decorated it may become an artist. The one who likes to make toys from scraps of wood may go on to develop his interest or could learn to hate woodworking if he is forced to make all his toys.

Encouraging creativity

When your child wants to know more about the rocks he has collected, help him discover the many places to get information: from books, other collectors, and through observation. When he's working on a project, leave him alone to solve the little problems he encounters. Provide him with the materials he needs if he can't come up with suitable substitutes. Let him experience occasional minor frustrations when he does things imperfectly; he'll experience the wonderful elation of success more when he finally does get the right solution.

Display the pictures he draws for you. Let him perform his original musical compositions. But, most importantly, judge his productions by standards he can understand and meet.

Give him a chance to use his imagination. Choose toys and playthings that can be used in many different ways. Let him have a say in arranging his room. Laugh at his jokes, but don't laugh when he comes dressed in one red sock and one blue one because he wants to match his striped shirt. Laugh with him when he proposes silly solutions to problems and knows they are silly, but help him see that his silly ideas aren't so terrible when he offers them seriously.

Let him know you value his ideas. Use them, when you can. If they are impossible, explain why and try to improve them together. Children who have good ideas and are encouraged to see them through to completion are more likely to have more good ideas.

Creative thinking can be discouraged. The family that cherishes conformity is not likely to value originality or nourish it. If only one right answer is accepted, the divergent thinker will refrain from searching for alternative answers. Where there is inflexibility about how to do things, where rigid standards of perfection are set for all endeavors without regard for their relative importance, creativity dies.

Creative people run by a different clock than do most of us. Often they cannot be dragged from their work; at other times they may show no interest in the very same project. Because they can be so exasperating, encouraging them is likely to require us to be enormously patient and understanding. But they are always exciting to be around and nurturing their creativity is usually well worth the effort.

ACHIEVEMENT

What influences a child of high mental ability to do something with that ability? Certainly learning and cognitive competence are not the only requirements for a successful life—ambition, opportunity, personality, and hard work go hand in hand with notable achievement.

Common sense tells us that potential for excellence is an essential for superior performance in any field. Just as it takes a certain body type to be world-class runner or a prima ballerina, excellence in the academic world requires higher than average intelligence. And in her study of eminent intellectual achievers, Catherine Cox uncovered three commonalities:

1. They were distinguished by behavior indicating high intellectual ability.

2. They were favored with a superior environment.

3. They were characterized by persistence of motive and effort, confidence in their ability, and strength of character.

Cox's last finding led other researchers to study the personality traits of high and low achievers. **Profound personality differences were noticed.** High achievers are goal oriented, more concerned with the future than the present, and can face failure while continuing to work toward a goal, willing to spend extra time in pursuit of that goal. They have a deep-seated self-confidence that is rooted in the early years and is hard to shake.

Success-oriented individuals look for ways to succeed. They are able to work independently, preferring situations in which they have personal responsibility. **High achievers seem driven to succeed.** They are interested in excellence for its own sake rather than the rewards it brings. Willing to take risks, they have high aspirations. As they experience success, they tend to raise their aspirations—failure only serves to increase their sense of reality.

These personality differences can be detected early and seem to have their roots in the home. Some are modeled after the parent. All can be nurtured as they appear.

MOTIVATION

The motivational theorists are generally divided into two camps: those who believe motivation comes from within and those who credit external circumstances. Perhaps, in the real world of child-rearing, you will find that **motivation is partly a function of what resides within the individual and partly a function of the environment.**

Intrinsic motivation is closely associated with values. It is relatively constant and hard to dull because it is not dependent on externals for prodding. The joy is in the doing. It is also related to self-concept, to the personal belief that efforts will have some effect.

The externals that have the greatest effect on the desire or drive to take action are anxiety, interest, success, and knowledge of the results of what we have done. A certain degree of anxiety can entice the individual to action, whereas too much will drive him away. You can influence your preschooler's motivation somewhat by regulating the amount of pressure he feels.

Children are attracted to interesting stimuli: the new, the uncertain, the humorous, the shocking. How many times have you used such stimuli to get your toddler to do something you wanted him to do?

Success lures learners to try more when that success is related to the difficulty of the task. (It is not nearly as fun to be successful at easy tasks as those offering a bit of a challenge!) Knowing how well they are doing also gives them an incentive for greater effort, so even failure—if only occasional and temporary—can motivate. Learners will keep on trying to do something difficult if they can see they are making progress toward their goal. Preschoolers can be motivated by this kind of feedback, and at their age, accurate, complete, and immediate feedback is the most meaningful.

USING THE BASICS

Most experts on child development assure us that it is within the ability of informed, aware, caring parents to provide their preschooler with a solid educational back-ground in the first few years so that he will be able to make the most of his experiences later in life.

The enormous responsibility of parenting cannot be denied. It is, at times, demanding and stressful; at others, rewarding and just plain fun. Your child's exceptionality, how-ever, adds another dimension to your task.

There are limits on just how much a parent can do for his child, but this should not keep you from doing what you can to create a climate in your home that will encourage his best possible development. You can do this by adding the basic information supplied in this chapter to that which you already possess on parenting in general and individualizing it all to fit your own situation.

The next several chapters of this book are devoted to specific learning activities for gifted children—activities you can adapt, for maximum effectiveness, to your particular needs. No book can plan an environment for you or prescribe specific activities that will be most nurturing for **your** gifted child. Only you can do that, because only you know what makes your situation unique.

7

Early Learning

The child learns more in his home during the preschool years than he does anywhere else in any other comparable period of his life. He learns through his interactions with his family and the stimulation of the physical environment. He gains the ability to relate to other people, laying the foundations of personal values and his feelings about his own worth. He develops physically while becoming the master of his senses. He learns direction and self-control. He grows intellectually and establishes patterns of learning that will continue through childhood and, probably, life.

The rate at which the gifted child learns is extraordinary. The way he explores and reacts to his environment is a marvelous phenomenon. For parents who facilitate this learning and growth there is nothing in life to compare with the adventure.

CHILDREN LEARN IMPORTANT THINGS IN THE FIRST FEW YEARS

Your preschooler is learning all day long, taking in impressions and sensations from the environment. What appear to be simple accomplishments all combine to prepare your child for a lifetime of learning. He is getting to know important things about the characteristics of the world and about his place in that world.

During the first few months, an infant expends most of his energy stockpiling information he gathers through sensory exploration of his environment and practicing new abilities as they emerge. Then, around the middle of the first year, signs of primitive intellectual behavior appear. When a baby moves his teddy bear out of the way so he can get to his ball, he is solving a problem. When you notice him showing signs of intention and anticipation, you are observing cognitive activity.

When your child starts to walk and talk, a whole new world is opened to him and he wants to experience every bit of it. While becoming less dependent on you for meeting many of his needs, still, **the kinds of things he learns during the next few years are inextricably bound to your attitudes and by the quality of the environment you provide for him.**

Learning through play

Whereas an infant gathers knowledge primarily through sensory impressions, a toddler learns through play. He loves to learn and goes at it with an intensity unlikely to be matched ever again. Play is a preschooler's work.

Through play, your child grows physically, emotionally, socially, and intellectually. Although there is overlap in the learning that takes place in these four areas of development, we will discuss each separately to give you some idea of the broad educational value of preschool play.

Physical

While your preschooler is running and jumping, climbing and tripping, he is learning how to manage his body—learning just what it can and cannot do. Play gives him a chance to practice his motor skills, skills he will use for the rest of his life. When he pokes and sniffs, handles and examines, he is sharpening his senses and learning how to use them to get information about his world. He is learning to use his senses more selectively, to see and hear specific things, to filter out unnecessary sensory stimuli. He is gaining control of his body.

Emotional

The same child who is learning to control his body is coincidentally trying to gain control of his emotions. Through his play activities he has the opportunity to try out a variety of responses and learn which work. He learns to express affection and annoyance in acceptable ways, to control his impulses, to deal with success and failure. He finds out what happens when he does what is expected of him and discovers the rewards of waiting his turn. Through role-playing activities and make-believe games he learns how it feels to be someone else and is able to release feelings or relive experiences. A gifted preschooler may exhibit unusual emotional development. For example, it is unusual for most children to show signs of empathy much before first or second grade, but some three-year-olds are able to put themselves in another's place. Also, because they are so aware of what is going on around them, gifted preschoolers sometimes learn to worry about things most little children shouldn't have to worry about. And, because they have an unusual sense of control over happenings, they can learn about guilt early, experiencing it in situations where they are convinced they may have caused something unpleasant to happen.

Social

The preschooler absorbs a variety of social skills and gets a chance to practice them in his play. As an infant he realizes how to get attention and hold it. From his caretaker he learns of the existence of authority and he discovers how to use others as resources when a task is too difficult for him. As he begins to spend more time within a peer group, he learns to get along with others—to share the spotlight, to compete, to react appropriately, and to develop effective leadership

behavior. Very soon he perceives cultural demands and discovers there are rules and standards he may not understand.
He becomes a social being and refines those skills that will
help him cope in the world beyond his front door in these
important preschool days.

Cognitive

Anyone can see how much a child grows in the first four or
five years. It is obvious and it is measurable. Maybe not so
obvious to the casual observer is the enormous growth in
intellectual behavior, the learning explosion, preschoolers
experience. This doesn't mean learning to name all the bones
in the body or reading **Gulliver's Travels** at four. It refers to
acquiring the important basics that will build a solid
foundation for all his future learning.

By the time your gifted child is ready to begin school, he
will already have learned the basics of the language into
which he was born. He will be amazingly proficient in using
language. He will understand subtle differences caused by
inflection and syntax and know so many words you would
probably have a hard time counting them!

When he first began to talk he mimicked the words he
heard; now he uses words as tools of thought. He learns more
and more words because he needs them and soon recognizes
the importance of using them correctly. As play becomes
increasingly complex, so does the vocabulary and the syntax.
"Run" no longer suffices when "I can run faster than you can"
is the game.

Through his play he learns to improvise, to find out how
things work and what fits into what, to use his body skillfully,
and to do for himself. He is motivated to notice details, make
associations and generalizations. Abstractions (past events,
colors, qualities, classes, concepts) become understandable.
The regularities in nature are noted and stored for future
reference; he becomes familiar with the physical world,
noticing when something is wrong or out of kilter with what
he already knows.

The preschooler is not limited to interacting with the
physical world. He can see things in his mind. Using his
imagination he can contemplate even the invisible, the non-

existent, and the vanished: an imaginary companion, fairies, and dinosaurs. He can invent new uses for old objects and new objects for old uses. He becomes a creator.

These years represent a most crucial period in a child's intellectual life, for he can be learning to learn and loving it. What better motivation for future learning can there be!

THE FIRST SIGNS OF LEARNING

From the moment of birth, your baby receives sensory information about his surroundings, but his first actions are simply reflexes: sucking, crying, grasping. It is not long, though, before he begins to gain some control over his actions and to discriminate among the sensations he receives.

In not too many weeks, you will notice he has begun paying attention to things for longer periods, imitating actions and sounds. Then comes intentional movement. When your baby gains limited control over his movement, he starts to explore and try to experience his effect on other things. He takes pleasure in repeating an action to see if it will get the same reaction over and over—trial-and-error learning begins. Through his senses and movement he is absorbing information and gradually learning to be more efficient in the information-gathering process.

Each child has his own rhythm for learning—his personal timetable—but all children apparently follow a similar pattern. They will concentrate on a new skill until they have mastered it and they will hold on to the familiar way of doing things until ready to take the next step. This explains why a child who is learning to walk will stop many of his other activities and concentrate fiercely on his walking, yet revert to crawling on occasion until he is secure in his newly acquired ability. But he is intent on learning to walk and there is nothing you can do to stop him from trying, just as it would have been impossible for you to "teach" him to walk earlier. There is an age before which a child cannot learn certain things—not the same age for all children, but this barrier does exist. If you want to help your child you will recognize this and then take your clues from him to determine when he can pick up new skills and learning. In the early years there is little need for formal instruction from you, but there are many other ways to help him learn.

TIPS ON TEACHING YOUR CHILD

- Focus on making your home a place where learning can take place, rather than on setting up a teacher-student relationship with your child.

- Don't worry about an elaborately enriched environment; just offer your child a variety of situations in which children can develop. He will choose the things he can deal with.

- Observe the skills that are emerging and provide opportunities for them to develop.

- Keep your explanations short and correct.

- Recognize your child's progress from skill to skill, giving help only when needed. Not all abilities need encouragement.

- Talk out loud when you are doing things—about how and why you do them a certain way.

- Speak to him in language close to—or slightly above—his apparent level of understanding. He learns more from speech that is directed at him than from listening to TV or records.

- Step back every once in a while and observe your own actions and reactions—he's learning something from them. Good? Or bad?

- React to his questions in the same vein they are offered. Serious questions deserve serious answers, whimsical ones do not.

- Enjoy his learning.

- Be patient—respect your child's natural limitations. Provide challenges he can meet.

- Respond to his overtures.
- Don't force him to learn. Tempt him.
- Telling is not teaching. Preschoolers learn by doing.
- Small children make no distinction between work and play.
- Your little learner needs parents who value the way he pokes and stacks, takes apart and puts together, looks and listens, examines and discovers.
- Plan to mesh the activities you arrange for him with his interests and his desire to learn.
- At first he will want approval for every job done, but once he is sure of himself he won't need it every step of the way. Don't be stingy with your approval, just sincere.
- It takes time to develop inner control. He needs your help.
- As he grows, give him more responsibility and a chance to make more decisions.
- Get out of his way. Don't be an obstacle to his learning. There is really no need to spend every minute interacting with a preschooler.
- Respect the importance of early learning. Don't try to make a six-year-old out of a two-year-old.
- Create an atmosphere conducive to play: time, materials, and approval.
- When possible, let him experience the consequences of his actions. While you certainly can't let him try out things that have unsafe consequences, or ones that he couldn't possibly anticipate, you can resist the temptation to point out obvious safe consequences.
- Recognize the tremendous influence parent expectations have on a child's learning, on the environment parents prepare, even on family interpersonal relationships.
- Sheltered children have less experience dealing with the unfamiliar, and all learning requires the ability to deal with the unfamiliar.

- Be sensitive to your child's behavior. Sometimes children act the way they do because they are at a certain stage of development.

- Children are influenced by the way questions are asked.

The parent-teacher wants to encourage the kinds of activities and provide an environment that will challenge the gifted child to high achievement. You must remember, though, that you are not your child's only teacher. He has many of them in the environment—some already present, and some you have arranged to be there.

WHAT MAKES A GOOD LEARNING ENVIRONMENT?

Sine your child is constantly absorbing information from his environment, you will want to provide the best surroundings you can. Sometimes seemingly minor changes in a young child's world will make an enormous difference in the kind of learning that can take place.

Let's examine some of the features that combine to make one environment more stimulating, more intellectually valuable, than another.

Most homes can be adapted, with a minimum of effort, to make an infant's small world interesting. What interests a baby? Sensory stimuli: things to see, hear, touch, taste, and smell. The stimuli should be changed frequently and the infant should be exposed to a variety rather than to a large quantity.

Your preschooler also requires an interesting environment for the best intellectual development, an environment that will become more personalized as he grows older. It will take more effort on your part to see that your preschooler's surroundings stimulate his intellectual growth than when he was an infant.

Little children haven't the slightest idea of what is good to learn and what is bad. They are not at all discriminating in this respect; they simply absorb whatever they find in their environment. It is up to the parent to make some choices during these early years.

Fundamental to a good learning environment is the positive atmosphere you create for your child. It should be one that is encouraging and nonjudgmental, in which your child feels free to experiment and make mistakes, where he has a sense of control but the element of surprise has not been removed, where independence is allowed gradually, and limits are clearly set.

The most valuable experiences and materials are those selected with his interests and ability in mind, but which will also expand his world. Opportunities should be planned for real-life experiences as well as make-believe in an uncluttered area in which he is not bound by excessive restrictions. The child should feel free to choose from among a variety of easily accessible materials and be given time to explore them to his satisfaction.

Every child should have balls and blocks, toys and games. All children need objects to manipulate, a world to explore, things about which to think. Your gifted child needs and learns from these same things. **However, there is a difference.** The gifted seem driven to "get more" from each experience.

Lists of games, toys, and reading materials can help you choose the things your child needs in his personal learning environment. There are books (see White, Gesell, and Montessori references in Chapter 5) describing activities appropriate for the preschooler in the home and publications and organizations (also see Chapter 5) advising parents on activities specifically appropriate for the gifted—rarely are the two combined. All these aids can be of value to you if you are creative in your choices of materials and activities, adapting the suggestions to your child's particular interests, needs, and ability. Let's explore some ways of making good ideas better so your child can get more mileage out of what he does.

Toys

Young children use toys to grow physically, mentally, and socially. Toys aid in developing coordination, large and small muscle control.

Toys can become "real" things and real things can be made into toys. A stack of blocks is a tower; one block, a car or a chair. Arranged carefully, they become a house, a cage, a fort, or something just to knock down. A bowl, in a child's hands, can be a hat or a drum, a container or a seat. A stick can be a horse or a sword. A little broom or a miniature hammer lets a youngster be, for a time, a grown-up. An old hat can open the doors to the land of make-believe.

A ball can be large or small, feel soft or hard. Some float, some sink, all fall when they are dropped. When bounced against a wall, they come back—sometimes. When he plays with his ball, do you think your child knows he is developing skills and learning valuable concepts he will use for the rest of his life? Of course not. Do you realize he is learning about buoyancy and gravity? Did you ever think that, years from now, because of his early experiences when he bounced a ball against the garage door, he will better understand that "the angle of incidence equals the angle of reflection"?

Your child will take apart his toys to see how they work and will put them back together to see if they **still** work. He will use them in the way the manufacturer intended, and he will discover clever new uses for them that the toymaker never imagined. **He does not need hundreds of toys; he needs interesting ones and he needs a variety.**

Games

The games you select for your child should be challenging —but not frustrating. They may require skill, concentration, memory, and the ability to follow directions. Games can teach number concepts and reward the observant, but they do not have to be "intellectual" to be educational. Some provide socializing opportunities: times together as a family, or an activity a gifted child can share with his age peers. Games demanding no particular skill still require taking turns. Games of chance teach the basics of the laws of probability, letting players take chances and risk failure, all in fun.

Your creative thinker will invent new games and try to improve on the old ones. He will experiment with the rules. You can encourage him to try new ones by playing them with him.

Books

You probably value books and reading, and already have many books in your home. You have undoubtedly seen that your child has a good supply. You read to him, encourage him to read, and know what interests him. There is no need to go into detail about the value and joys of reading, but a few points should be made.

Be flexible. When you are reading to your young child and find he does not like the book or is not at all interested in it, by all means put it away or skip to a more interesting part. Reading should not be a chore looked upon as something that must be finished no matter what—not all books **must** be read straight through. (It is surprising how many gifted students do not know this fact.)

You can show your child the tricks you use to decide if you want to read a book, such as looking for books by a favorite author or those with detailed illustations. Some readers prefer "fat" books, some hate small print. Many people read every book on the best-seller lists, others select only the most shopworn books on the library shelves. Many detective story readers skim the last page before deciding if they want to read the whole book. You should teach him the library skills he needs to find the books he wants and can explain the different uses of books: such as reading for pleasure, for specific knowledge, for relaxation, or just for something to talk about.

If your little reader has difficulty, as so many do, finding a book on his reading level, you can teach him the trick many primary teachers use. Some call it the "Rule of Thumb." Have his start reading on a page near the middle of the book and each time he comes to a word he does not know, he is to hold up one finger. If he comes to his thumb before the end of the page, the book is too hard.

Most children, with a little help, are able to find plenty of books on the things that interest them. You should make an effort, though, to see that your reader also has access to good books on other topics, on things he has not yet gotten around to thinking about. Choose books that excite your child's imagination, get him involved, or give him honest information. Read E. B. White's **Charlotte's Web** to your child, laugh and cry with him, share his delight in the sound of the prose.

Let your preschooler enjoy the illustrations that make Munro Leaf's **Ferdinand** an all-time favorite. Be selective when choosing informative books such as a children's encyclopedia; the facts and illustrations should be clear, correct, and sufficient for your child's interests and ability. Share your old favorites as well as your new finds.

In most libraries you will find two excellent references. **The Horn Book Magazine** is a periodical, published every two months, which is devoted to children's literature, and Mary Hill Arbuthnot's **Children and Books** can be used as a source for new book ideas. Some of the gifted organizations listed in Chapter 5 have compiled lists of favorites. You can write for them at the addresses given.

Activities

You can also obtain lists of suggested activities appropriate for the gifted child from the organizations named in Chapter 5. Take these suggestions and, using your knowledge about the gifted in general together with the basics from Chapter 6, devise some really valuable activities suitable for **your** child and **your** circumstances. An informed parent will not follow any book blindly, no matter how good it is or how full of great ideas. Both you and your child are individuals and have your own likes and dislikes, needs and values, time and resources.

Use such books for reference, much as you use your cookbook. You wouldn't think of starting at the beginning of a cookbook and going straight through preparing each recipe in turn—you would end up with a strange diet indeed! Instead, you choose an assortment of foods based on your knowledge of good nutrition and use the cookbook as a reference to give you ideas on how to prepare the foods you and your family need and enjoy. For variety, you try new recipes. You discard the ones you don't like, repeat some of your favorites, and make adjustments to suit your individual tastes. And, you are careful not to overeat. (As one mother said after a parent-teacher workshop on gifted children, "I thought I was going to O.D. on good ideas!")

Let's see how four suggestions from a typical list of activities for gifted children can be expanded or adapted to fit your particular situation.

1. "Go to the library." You do not just "go" to a library with a gifted child. A library can be confusing, overwhelming—much like too many toys on Christmas morning. Take it a little at a time, and **go with a purpose.** Go in search of a book on dinosaurs, or another book by the author of one of your child's favorites, or take a trip one day just to explore. By all means, get to know the librarian—one librarian. Let your child have talks with her so she will know your child, his interests and ability. Your preschooler will not only get help in book selection, but will learn a valuable lesson: how to use books and people as resources.

2. "Talk and listen to your child." This is good advice for any parent, especially if you think about the **quality** of your communications with your child. When you talk to him, use the correct words. He might say "choo-choo," but you can still say train—he will know what you mean. And when he is around three, when that so-called vocabulary explosion takes place, use words such as locomotive, and diesel, and steam-driven; you will be amazed at how easily he picks up these new words.

There are so many ways to communicate so many ideas, and he learns from you. Make your message specific to the situation and sufficiently detailed when you talk to him. How much more he learns from your saying "Don't open the door, the flies will get into the house," than from a simple "Stop!" Do you want him to clean his room, straighten up that messy room, or merely to put his toys away? Be precise.

Consider the mental response to your communications. If you avoid using questions that require a simple "yes" or "no" answer, you will find yourself asking ones that will make him think rather than just react. Similarly, suppose an important news bulletin comes on the air and he is trying to get your attention at the same time. You can say "Hush" or "Wait until this is over; I want to hear this message." How much more he can learn from the latter. By complying he is respecting the wishes of others and waiting his turn. He must also make a judgment: deciding whether what he has to say is more important than what you might hear on the broadcast. You hope he will have enough sense to persist if he wants to tell you the stew is boiling over, and he is more likely to interrupt to give you such a message if he has had practice making this kind of judgment than if he has been conditioned to "hush" on command.

You can discover so many important things about your child just by listening to what he has to say. You'll learn about his feelings and interests, about his perceptions and misconceptions, about his ability and his growth. Most gifted children are very sensitive to the difference between listening and merely hearing. Be an active listener. React to what your child has to say. Ask questions when you miss his point. Gifted chilren begin playing with words very early. They tease, kid, and banter. They say things intended to get reactions. If you are not really listening, your reaction will probably be inappropriate and you will both miss out on this delightful game.

It is not only important for you to listen to him, but for you to let him speak for himself. Let him order his own Big Mac and milk. Wait for him to tell the pediatrician how he is feeling. Resist the temptation to put words into his mouth; give him time to search for just the right one. If you know a better word, use it in your response. "Yes, that car is a nice **bronze** color."

3. "Travel." Do not skip this suggestion just because you know your family cannot take a year to tour the world. The value in travel with a preschooler is in the exposure to different sorts of people and various aspects of human culture and in the opportunity to sharpen the observation and communication skills he will need to benefit from later traveling experiences. **The distance traveled is not important.** It is not necessary to go to Florence to see fine art, to Brazil to hear a foreign language, or to India to see poverty. Look for things to do and places to visit in your own area. Go exploring.

4. "Allow your child liberty on the unimportant things." A great idea for starters, but **your gifted child will soon catch on if he is allowed to decide only the unimportant things.** Letting him decide whether to wear the blue or the red socks is a good technique to use in the beginning, but this type of decision is too limited. Your goal should be that he will eventually be able to make complex decisions. You help him deal with greater complexity by gradually increasing the factors he must consider. In his choice of clothing, for

example, he may well start with a decision based simply on color preference, but he should soon have the opportunity to give some thought to other factors, such as the weather, the appropriateness of the outfit to the occasion, and what he will be doing. He'll probably make a few bad decisions; it's not the end of the world. Recognize his attempts, do not condemn his failures. Increase the importance of the decisions he is to make as his ability to deal with them grows.

In an atmosphere in which all family members are encouraged to make informed choices and are not criticized for mistakes, your child will grow up a secure decision-maker, free to take the risks demanded of him, able to face the consequences of his choices.

By the time your child reaches school age, he will have absorbed a tremendous amount of information about the world around him. He will have acquired most of the skills he will need to benefit from later formal instruction—having learned how to learn—and will have formed very fundamental perceptions about his own ability to function. Your efforts can have a significant impact on the amount and quality of his early learning. It's an exciting prospect and it can be fun!

8

The Three R's at Home

There is no reason why you cannot teach your gifted child the three R's before he goes to school—if he wants to learn. Reading, writing, arithmetic, science, and social studies interest gifted preschoolers, and when these subjects are presented in a way that is compatible with your young child's limited experience, meaningful learning occurs.

The average home provides more than adequate opportunities for learning and parents have proved themselves to be phenomenally successful teachers. Most preschool learning takes place in the home, is facilitated by the parent, and is not consciously structured. The kind and amount of learning is determined essentially by when, what, and how much the individual child wants to learn. The pace is set by the learner rather than the teacher.

Ideally, during these preschool years you will fashion an environment in which your child **develops a positive attitude**

toward learning, concentrating on laying a solid educational foundation rather than devoting time to seeing how much your child can learn.

READING

The controversy over when is the best time to teach a child to read is a source of anxiety for many parents. You find some educators demonstrating their successes in teaching infants to read, while other highly respected authorities avow that it is best to postpone beginning reading instruction as long as possible. Part of the reason for this large discrepancy lies in a fundamental philosophical disagreement (Is reading the best use of a toddler's time?) and part is based in semantics (What, precisely, is reading?).

What is reading?

Since definitions of reading vary widely, judgments about when a child first reads can differ enormously, depending on which definitions are used. The definitions range from the mere act of recognition or simple decoding to a most sophisticated involvement with ideas. Is a three-year-old reading if he recognizes his name in a book? Or is it reading when a five-year-old picks up **Stuart Little** and dissolves in laughter at the mouse's antics?

If you can accept that reading is an extension of learning to talk and listen, then you should be comfortable with the idea that reading goes beyond simply the saying of words to **a process of deriving meaning from printed symbols.** If you can see that it is not a matter of being a nonreader one day and a reader the next, you will understand that reading is a **developmental process** requiring a certain maturity and some reasoning ability.

Is your child ready to read?

There is a great deal more to the complex act of reading than mere mouthing of words or uttering of certain sounds in response to visual clues. It entails a mental response to print by the reader. Mastery of the act is facilitated by the possession of certain prerequisite skills that relate to the learner's understanding of what reading is all about: that ideas can be communicated through visual symbols and that changes in either the symbols or their order result in a change in the message. These prereading skills, listed below, are those your child will need to become a successful reader. They are important and they come first.

PREREADING SKILLS CHECKLIST

_____ Can relate to characters and situations in books.

_____ Remembers stories he has heard.

_____ Can anticipate what comes next in a story.

_____ Notices changes you make when reading.

_____ Able to tell stories with a beginning, middle, and end.

_____ Able to draw information from a picture.

_____ Can arrange a set of pictures in story order.

_____ Shows interest in signs and symbols.

_____ Understands that printed words communicate messages.

_____ Is familiar with format of books.

_____ Understands that we read the print and not the pictures.

_____ Aware that print is read from left to right, top to bottom.

_____ Knows that a page of print takes longer to read than a single line.

_____ Can focus attention on story being read.

_____ Aware of the sounds in language and can match sounds.

_____ Can discern likenesses and differences in patterns and designs.

_____ Can recognize letters as parts of words.

If your very bright preschooler has not begun to read books, it does not necessarily mean that he is not smart or that there is something wrong. There are factors other than intellectual that affect the ability to read; some are maturational. For instance, most preschoolers have a tendency toward farsightedness and have difficulty focusing on a near point for extended periods. Some children have not yet developed a strong enough sense of knowing they can do for themselves—and reading is one act no one else can do for them. There could be any number of perfectly legitimate reasons, but I would suspect that if your child has mastered most of the basic skills listed, you might find that he is indeed reading. **Your child does not have to be able to read books to be a reader!**

How do you teach someone to read?

First of all you do **not** go out and buy one of those books that guarantee your two-year-old will be reading everything in the house in just a few short weeks. Even if it were possible, there is so much more for a young child to do and learn, which will be neglected if he has his nose stuck in a book.

Second, you do **not** sit down one day and teach, rather you remember that children learn with enthusiasm in a supportive atmosphere in which their interests and rate of learning receive primary consideration.

You **do** three things:

1. You read to your child.
2. You expose him to print.
3. You give him the help he needs.

Read to your child as often as possible.

All sorts of good things come from this one simple activity. Most importantly, it gives you and your child time together with all the implications that has in his total development. In addition, he will absorb so many things that will influence his later success as a reader.

A child who is read to learns that reading is enjoyable and that books are filled with interesting things. He learns what reading is all about: print and pictures can represent ideas and things; books are read from the beginning to the end, from left to right, top to bottom. When you say exactly the same words every time you read his favorite story, he soon gets the idea that there is a connection between what he sees and what he hears. He picks up the ability to listen with a purpose and to pay attention, to follow the sequence of a story and to remember details. Books can enlarge his vocabulary and extend his environment. From hearing stories read, he builds a storehouse of language patterns and possibilities beyond those which he hears in his immediate environment and he begins to anticipate the next idea or word. When there are no pictures, he is encouraged to develop visual images.

If you take the time to talk about what you have read, being careful not to make it a session requiring him to answer questions, he will also learn something some people never learn: responsive reading (to read critically, to think about what the printed word means, to ask questions, and to make judgments about the content of what he has read).

Provide an environment rich in a variety of printed materials.

Let him see that you own and enjoy your books and magazines; give him some of his own. Encourage him to notice words around him: on cereal boxes and billboards, labels and signs, trucks and buildings, and, of course, on TV. Reinforce the concept that reading constitutes a meaningful part of our lives by showing him how helpful written words can be when cooking, using a new appliance, learning the rules for a new game, finding the right street, or recording thoughts.

Label his possessions and some common objects around the house if he shows an interest. To build his understanding that print is just talking put on paper, let him dictate letters to his friends and relatives, label his artwork or ask him if he wants you to help write about what he has drawn in his picture. Leave messages for him on the refrigerator door, on his pillow, or on his chalkboard. These first messages should make use of pictures, shapes, or colors to communicate your message (learning to interpret symbols is one step toward learning to read print).

Help him in his efforts to learn to read.

Your gifted child is observant and curious; soon he will be asking what something says or for help in labeling his own pictures. Pay attention to what his is beginning to do and provide opportunities for him to practice. When he notices similarities and differences in words and letters, encourage him. Direct him to make comparisons. When he can recognize a letter or a word, let him practice finding it on billboards or in books. When he can hear that words such as "play" and "day" rhyme, play rhyming games. Call attention to words that begin alike or in the same way as his name. Play games that require listening for specific sounds, such as a particular bird's call or one instrument in an orchestra, so that when he begins to read he will be able to distinguish the sounds in words and be more able to make the connection between the printed symbol and the way it is pronounced.

Write down things your child says and read them aloud to him. If he tries to read them back to you, you need not worry if his version is not exactly right. Some children learn to read by "reading" their favorite story over and over, each time getting closer to the way it is written in the book. It can be fun to learn to read in a nonthreatening situation, where a child's favorite person helps him.

WRITING

Many children who start reading before they enter school, learn to read and write simultaneously. There is a close bond between the two abilities; the learning of one facilitates the learning of the other.

Your child's first writing might look like scribbles to you, but these early attempts are very similar to the way he played with sounds in his crib. That was the first step to speech, and his first scribbles will lead to writing.

The first word most children want to write is their own name. Say the letters as you write them for him to copy and he will soon be practicing these few letters and using them to "write" all sorts of things. He will experiment, making up some of his own letters to go with the ones he already knows.

Although it is not necessary to know the names of the letters of the alphabet to learn to read, it makes it much easier for you to help your child write a word he wants if he knows a "d," and an "o," and a "g." Teach the letters to him as he needs them.

Do not worry about whether to use capital (R) or lowercase (r) letters; he will have to know them both eventually. (Many first-grade teachers insist the students use lowercase, because of its similarity to the print in books.) It is likely the preschool learner will pick up the capitals first, however, because so many of the first things he reads are written in capitals: STOP, SLOW, MR. COFFEE, BRAN FLAKES. But many observant children soon notice there are two ways to write letters and learn them simultaneously. Some children even notice that many letters look a little different printed in books than the way they write them.

Encourage his interests, answer his questions, show him the accepted ways to write, and do not criticize his attempts. Just as we do not expect our two-year-olds to speak in complete sentences, so we should not expect a preschooler's first attempts at recording an idea to be free from error or even to make sense.

ARITHMETIC

Many parents are quite comfortable teaching their preschoolers to count and to add and subtract, and they are quite successful in their efforts. Yet, if your intention is to cultivate a strong mathematical base for future learning, there are important fundamental concepts to which you will want to expose your child—concepts such as more and less, the difference between four and fourth, the meaning of zero, among others.

A very difficult concept for most children to comprehend is time: past, present, the future, the sequence of happenings, duration, and the continuousness of time. Part of the problem is that time is perceived differently by all of us. How long is a minute in a mother's "wait a minute" or just when was a "long time ago" to a three-year-old. A year is an enormous part of a preschool child's life, yet it may seem very little to an octogenarian. Clocks and calendars hold a special fascination for the gifted; use them to help him gain a better sense of time. Play games estimating time: guess how long will it take to do something, or set a timer and try to finish a project before the buzzer goes off.

Besides estimating time, your gifted child can learn some important concepts by estimating distance, weight, and other measures. It can be fun checking how close his estimates are to the actual measure. Do not feel bound to using conventional measures (feet, pounds, hours, meters). "How many steps do you think it is from this chair to the nurse's desk?" "How many paper clips weigh the same as this pencil?" "How many scoops of sugar will it take to fill this sugar bowl?"

Children can learn many difficult mathematical concepts through actual manipulation of materials. One-to-one relationships become clear to a preschooler who pairs the clean socks in the wash or who is responsible for placing one napkin at each dinner place. Play with blocks and balls and clay can foster the learning of comparative terms such as small, smaller, smallest; longer or shorter; heavier and lighter; small, medium, large; one-half. An understanding of volume will come more easily to a child who has access to jars and cups, sand, water, and clay. Feeling the difference between a ball and a block precedes visual recognition of the differences among the many geometric shapes. Even the very difficult task of ordering (by qualities such as shape, size, shades of color) can be approached with some success by gifted children in their everyday work/play experiences manipulating commonplace materials.

Math is more than memorizing the times tables, and numerous instructive experiences are available to a preschool child who has the advantage of an environment rich in opportunities for learning.

SCIENCE

Your goal in exposing your child to various scientific experiences is not to teach him the things he will be expected to learn later in a classroom, nor is it to make a scientist of him; it is rather to familiarize him with the **scientific approach,** a way of looking at the world and learning from it. Based on the skills of observation, prediction, experimentation, and interpretation, this method is particularly suited to the gifted learner. To be an effective teacher, however, you should be aware of the three factors that affect a child's progress in the scientific field: maturation, experience, and education.

Maturation

When a very young child first reaches out to understand his world, the information he amasses is limited to that which he gains through his senses. He struggles to bring order to the kinds of information he receives. But, because of his limited experience and the fallibility of sensory perceptions, many of the conclusions he reaches contradict each other. It is only as the child matures that he becomes able to deal with apparent contradictions and find ways to explain them.

To help you understand the role maturity plays in a child's perception of happenings, try this experiment with several children, ages two, five, and twelve. All you need is a coin to learn a great deal about a child's conception of the permanence of objects.

Palming the Coin* After showing a coin to a child, put your hands behind your back and conceal the coin in one hand. Present your two clenched fists to the child and ask him to guess which hand the coin is in. Open the fist he selects. If the coin is not in that hand, close it and open the other to reveal the coin. After repeating this procedure two or three times, leave the coin behind your back and present two **empty** fists to the child.

What happens next will give you insight into the different ways children of varying maturities approach problems. The youngest child, not finding the coin in the second fist, will go back to the first expecting it to be there after all. The five-

---

*This experiment is based on the observations of Swiss psychologist Jean Piaget.

year-old is likely to express confusion and ask what happened to the coin. While the more mature twelve-year-old will either assume you cheated or will look behind you for the coin.

Experience

The major part of a preschooler's scientific learning occurs in an **unstructured atmosphere in which the child is actively involved with materials that demonstrate the laws of nature.** It is through his perceptions of the regularities he finds in nature that the young child is able to make certain generalizations and predictions. By repeated experiences with clay, for instance, a child comes to the realization that the mass remains the same even when the shape changes. As he plays with magnets, lenses, prisms, balance scales, musical instruments, blocks, and the simple machines, he learns about their functions. Even as he plays with sand and water, paints and cloth, records and food, he is building a vocabulary that helps him make finer and finer distinctions in his sense impressions: the visual properties of size, shape, and color; the pitch and intensity of sounds; words of touch such as hot, rough, soft, or sharp; bitter or sweet taste sensations; the different variations of odor from sweet to rotten, from pleasant to those that signal danger. Through these kinds of hands-on experiences, a preschooler builds up a kind of intuitive understanding of the concepts that will serve him through the years.

Education

Your child's understanding of scientific concepts can be broadened and his factual knowledge increased when you borrow some simple instructional techniques from the teaching profession.

There are three basic methods a science teacher uses in the classroom: the lecture or demonstration, student experiments, and required reading. The successful teacher knows when to use each method.

Lectures and demonstrations are common methods of passing knowledge to the student. The teacher must, however, take care to use language and examples that are appropriate to the students' ages and backgrounds. Your preschooler will more easily assimilate new facts that you relate to other things he knows and he will be more likely to add new scientific terms to his vocabulary when you introduce them in terms consistent with his present level of understanding.

Spoon-feeding a plethora of information to a child is not wise. But, many times, the most efficient way for him to learn something is simply to be told. It is not necessary for a learner to make every discovery for himself. For example, your preschooler should not have to wait until he can read a medical book to know it was his "tibia" he hurt when he fell. Nor should he have to wait until he is drowning to learn about the force of an undertow.

When your child needs information fast, give it to him. When he is in the middle of a creative production is **not** the time for instruction. "What can I use to make this piece of foam stick to this pipe?" should elicit a quick "The glue I use for my crafts," rather than a long lesson on the properties of bonding materials.

A science teacher will usually choose to assign an experiment when there is a scientific principle to be learned. Your preschooler will absorb much more information concerning the principle of buoyancy through "experimenting" with objects that float or sink than if you tell him which of his toys will float and why. There are, of course, some experiments you would not let a youngster try because they would be dangerous. If this is the case, you might consider a demonstration.

Often all that is required of you as a parent-teacher is an ability to direct your child's attention to specific phenomena, asking what happened, why, and will it happen again. When problems occur in his life, encourage him to find solutions using his skills of observation and prediction. Give him opportunities to try out his solutions and time to decide why he may or may not have been successful—it is not the answers he gets so much as the way he goes about getting them that counts.

Teachers use science books to interest students in the new or the unusual, to teach them how to gather needed information, and to supply background or supporting materials. Fortunately, today's science books for young children are becoming more attractive and publishers are putting a great deal of emphasis on presenting scientific facts in an honest and palatable format. Books on plants and animals, the human body, space, natural phenomena, and the like belong on your bookshelf within easy reach.

SOCIAL STUDIES

The broad goal of a school social studies curriculum is to encourage the student to become a contributing member of society. Learning about other people is fundamental to this concept. Children should understand that individuals differ, how others live and work, how to resolve conflicts, and the reasons for rules.

Children can learn about other times and other peoples even without the chronological perspective of adults. They deal comfortably with historical events by thinking of them as "long ago" as opposed to "now."

Also included in the broad concept of social studies are specific skills in map reading, ordering events in time, and critical thinking. These skills are **extremely difficult** for most preschoolers but some gifted children display a competence in these areas early. When you are guiding your preschooler, keep in mind that he sees events more clearly as they relate to him. For example, beginning map reading skills can be introduced by drawing a plan of your child's room and enlisting his help in positioning the furniture, doors, and windows. Then there can be a gradual, natural progression from his room to house plans, lot plans, and neighborhood maps.

Simple time lines centering on your child's life can help him understand the relationships of some chronological events (see Chapter 9 for how to make a time line). Shopping trips and TV commercial viewing present innumerable opportunities to awaken critical thinking skills. Don't let exaggerated advertising claims get by without making some sort of comment. Let your child see you resist the impulse to buy something just because of attractive packaging or display. Let him participate in some of the many decisions you make concerning product size, need, usefulness, and the like. Relevant experiences are not so difficult to find, if you are looking for them.

LEARNING AT HOME

Your gifted child can learn about everything he finds interesting. Learning can be fun, not a chore, in the absence of pressure, when a child is allowed to make mistakes. Start with easy concepts and tasks. Build success into his learning experiences by beginning with what he already knows and stopping when things become too hard or when he loses interest. Enjoy the experience with him. **He does not have to learn everything there is to learn today, this week, or even this year!**

You have definite advantages over a classroom teacher: you can pursue your child's interests; you are not required to follow a predetermined curriculum, nor are you restricted by an inflexible schedule; and, most importantly, you can give individual attention to your child's needs and progress.

You are also in a position to decide which experiences make the best use of his preschool years. You can observe his behavior to determine the kinds of experiences he needs to aid in his healthy development. You can give him interesting things to manipulate and explore. You can answer his questions and introduce him to new ideas while providing him opportunities to put these new ideas to work. You can see that he has a broad base of experience and knowledge so he will benefit from later educational experiences. **What your child will learn in the future is a function of how and what he is learning today.**

9

Starters

Researchers report two important observations about the learning characteristics of gifted children: 1) The experiences they have in their first few years—even before differences in ability become apparent—are predominantly those that foster the development of the skills of observation, communication, information gathering, and decision-making; and 2) as they mature, these children seem to have the ability to absorb more learning from any given set of circumstances than their average playmates.

The purpose of this chapter is to exhort you to take advantage of these facts. It alerts you to the **opportunities for valuable learning that constantly present themselves in your child's everyday life** and gives you some idea of the kinds of activities through which your gifted child can expand his knowledge base. These activities are called starters because they are intended only to get you started providing the kind of environment that will stimulate your child's giftedness.

One of your major educational objectives in these preschool years, while you still have some degree of control over the kinds of experiences to which your child is exposed, will be to **give him a variety of things to think about.** But do not despair if you are unable to see immediate evidence of great thinking. You are, after all, only planting the seeds—not all of them will sprout at the same time.

Consider the simple project of making a parachute. The entire activity—from the gathering of materials, to assembling them, to playing with the finished product—will take probably less than an hour. Then your child will go on to other things. However, one day, you may find him busily constructing a **better** parachute on his own, taking into account differences in fabrics and making allowances for the effects of a breeze, perhaps even devising an ingenious method to project the parachute into the air. Or you might find him totally absorbed in a book about Leonardo daVinci. Could that simple little parachute have been the seed that produced all this later learning.

In approaching any learning activity for your preschooler, your emphasis should be on the **exposure** rather than teaching, on the child **doing** rather than watching. Keep offering more, then back off so that your child's ability to create his own intellectual experiences will transcend his need to receive stimulation from others.

These starter activities are not intended to be followed like a prescription. Read through them for ideas you can creatively adapt to your own family's interests, resources, and abilities.

Have you thought of going to the local high school to hear the concert band practice? Or would your preschooler enjoy sitting in the empty bleachers to watch the marching band go through its routine? There are some real advantages in visiting the high school bands over attending a community concert in a hall. The concerts at the school can be attended right after naptime rather than after bedtime. You can talk about the music without worrying about disturbing anyone, and you can leave when you and your child have had enough. And, they are free!

There are wonders to be found in an ordinary sandbox! One plus one does not always make two! When you mix one cup of sand with one cup of water, what do you get? What happened? Why? A steady drip of water can wear quite a crevice in a sand hill. And look! The second and third drips are following the path of the first.

A whole neighborhood can be built in a sandbox—with roads and houses and parks and whatever we want. Why if you stand way back, it looks just like a map!

Scrapbooks are interesting to put together and it is fun to write something about each entry.

Art museums are not the only places to find works of art. Try an art supply store or go to a fair. You can frequently find paintings and pieces of sculpture on display in local restaurants, colleges, civic buildings, even in the homes of friends who have collected some art reproductions or originals.

Visit an artist's studio one day. Most have their work for sale and are happy to let the public browse. Call first.

Borrow prints from your library. Cut pictures from old magazines and mount them. Paint your own.

Discuss your likes and dislikes with your preschooler. Talk about the different techniques, the use of color, and even a little about perspective.

Sometimes give very specific directions to be followed step by step.

Kitchens are full of opportunities to . . . measure, match, and count . . . learn new words and use all five of your senses . . . make estimates and confirm good guesses . . . follow directions and be creative.

Make some musical instruments and play them. Stretch various sized rubber bands around a topless cigar box and pluck them. Seal dried beans in a small box and shake it. Pour water into some glasses to different levels, then tap the glasses gently with a spoon. Make a drum out of an oatmeal box. Any two sticks can become tapsticks. Hum through a piece of tissue paper wrapped around a comb. Put on a record or turn on the radio and march or play in time to the music.

Ask questions to encourage the use of as many senses as possible to make observations and to gain information.

"What is that I smell? Where is it coming from?" "Did you hear that noise? Shh, listen carefully." "What's that hum? Could it be the refrigerator?" "Can you see if the cookies are cool yet?" "How can we tell if this tea has been sweetened?"

A paper towel tube can become a rocket . . . with some paint, stiff paper, and paste.

Make a family tree using photographs of all the members.

A large, inexpensive bulletin board can be made from smooth nonacoustical ceiling paneling. It comes in various sizes, but a piece two by four feet will hold quite a number of your child's drawings, notes, special mementos, and favorite photographs. Most building supply stores and some large variety stores carry these panels.

Bead stringing helps develop better eye-hand coordination and is great fun. Preschoolers like to make jewelry, and to arrange patterns and copy them. Some children enjoy stringing pieces of macaroni—which they have painted—onto shoe laces or on string that has had one end dipped in paraffin.

Take a walk. Take lots of them. Explore the world with your preschooler. Stoop down and let your child-guide point out the little creeping and crawling things. Take time to wonder together about the things you see.

Lie on your back in the green grass and watch the summer clouds put on their kaleidoscopic show.

Fill a shoebox with interesting scientific equipment just for your little scientist. You might include a magnifying glass, a prism, some magnets, an arm-balance scale, a mirror, a compass (keep this away from the magnets), some small jars with caps, a set of measuring spoons, some rubber bands and small squares of cheesecloth, and an eyedropper.

Play games that require the players to pay attention to observable qualities. In games such as "I Spy" and "Teapot," the players take turns describing an object in plain view for the other players to guess.

"I spy something brown, with four legs, and it has dishes on it. What is it?"

Answer: a table

"I see a teapot. It is round and red and rolls when it is pushed. What is it?"

Answer: a ball

Have you ever watched a caterpillar walk or an ice cube melt?

Does your child have a dress-up box filled with old hats and shoes, jewelry, shirts and skirts, feathers and belts, dresses and coats? Any old box will do, but there must be enough variety in the assortment of costumes so your child, and his friends, can become any number of different characters by changing items of clothing.

Turn off the television.

Find opportunities for your child to put objects into groups, first by one observable quality (such as size, color, form), then move gradually to more complicated tasks. After your child can put all the red blocks into one box and the green ones into another and can arrange the small blocks on the top shelf, the large on the bottom, then he will be ready to tackle a task such as putting all the little purple beads into one cup, the big yellow ones into another, and all the rest into the bucket.

However, before a child can group things by observable qualities, he must have experience observing them. Let him play with the beads, handle them, and get to know them first.

Encourage your child to make his own toys. When he is very young he will have the knack of turning any object you give him into a plaything; you need only to keep this imaginative ability alive. Show your approval when he makes a long cardboard tube become a horse, when a towel transforms him into a superhero, or when some wood, a stick, and a piece of cloth sail to a distant shore.

Take turns making up new endings to old stories.

Give your preschooler one of those large mail order catalogs some departments stores distribute. There are thousands of new words to be learned thumbing through those pages and there are hundreds of pictures to be cut out and pasted onto a piece of paper or used to decorate a special box.

Show your child the world . . . starting with interesting places near his home: the firehouse, the bakery, the library, a museum, a construction site, an old old tree . . .

Take time to talk to the firemen, the baker, the librarian, a docent, a hard-hat, an old old man . . .

Discover board games the whole family can play together. One costs less than the price of a movie or a trip to a fast food restaurant, and the game will last for years.

Have you ever seen a monarch butterfly in your neighborhood? You might be able to share an incredibly beautiful experience with your child if the monarchs do come through your area. Ask your country agricultural agent, a representative of a local garden club, or one of the science teachers at your neighborhood school where you might find some milkweed, the plant on which the female monarch lays her tiny eggs.

Your child can view the whole metamorphic process—from larva to chrysalis to butterfly—by taking a few branches of milkweed on which the eggs have been laid and placing them in a simple cardboard box with a piece of screening taped over one side.

Picture dictionaries are loved by beginning readers and writers.

The child who helps with the laundry can be learning many valuable concepts. When your preschooler helps you sort the wash into piles of white items and colored items, or darks, lights, and whites, he is actually grouping by observable qualities. While he may not yet be able to fold the tee shirts perfectly, if he can put Dad's clothing in one pile and his own in another, he has already added an abstract quality (ownership) to the grouping task.

When your preschooler arranges his clean clothes in the proper drawers, it should not really matter terribly that the job he does is not as neat as you might do. He is doing much more than just being helpful, he is practicing mental skills that will serve him well in the future.

Sometimes give general instructions rather than specific directions; then let your child figure out how to comply.

"Find a box that we can use to carry these books to Jimmy's house," rather than "Get the white box from my closet." "Put Mother's birthday present someplace she'll see it when she first walks into the house," rather than "Put this present on the kitchen table." "What can we put under this plant so it won't stain the table?" rather than "Put this dish under that plant."

A child who has his own little tool box and some scraps of wood can enjoy many valuable educational experiences. He can learn to measure, to compare sizes and shapes, to match, to plan a project, and to execute his plan. In the process of having fun he will be practicing the important coordination between his eyes and his hands and will be fostering the development of both the large and small muscles he will need for more complicated tasks later. And, best of all, with his tool box, wood, and a little imagination, he can make all sorts of wonderful things!

Gardens are fun and everyone can have one. They teach a child responsibility and about some of the wonders of living things. It is easy to sprout alfalfa seeds (gotten from a health food store) and they make any salad a little better. Just put a couple of tablespoonfuls of sprouting seeds into a large-mouth jar over which you have secured a piece of screening. Soak them for a few hours, then, after pouring the water out, turn the jar on its edge in a bowl so the excess moisture can drain out, then cover them with a cloth. Twice a day for the next few days, rinse the seeds by filling the jar with fresh water and shaking gently. Pour the rinse water out and replace the jar in the bowl. Recover. Before the end of a week, your sprouts will be ready to put on sandwiches and in salads.

Seeds from your breakfast orange or grapefruit can be grown in your kitchen window. After soaking a few of the seeds overnight, plant three or four of them in a container of potting soil. In a few weeks little plants will appear, and you can watch your citrus grow.

Peas or beans are large and easy for a preschool youngster to handle. They are easy to grow, come up fast, and make a nice vine that can be placed in a child's bedroom window for him to watch.

It is hard to keep some potatoes from sprouting. Suspend one on toothpicks in a colored jar (to protect the roots from the light) and your preschooler can watch the roots grow as fast as the vine.

Carrot tops, avocado seeds, bulbs, and radish seeds can also be grown easily at home by your preschool gardener.

Did you know that you can make a picture of one cat turn into a picture of two? Or make a small box large? Or a large hourse small? If you hold a hand mirror up against a picture and tilt it just so, you can do all sorts of magical things.

As soon as he is able, send him on errands.

Some older preschoolers can handle a camera quite successfully. If your child shows an interest in photography, you might consider getting him an inexpensive simple camera of his own. With it he will be able to capture memorable moments, take photographs for the family album, and keep records of a project. He will learn to be responsible for an important piece of equipment, to wait for results, that directions must be followed carefully, and possibly become familiar with some basics of composition. He might even learn to judge which things are worth capturing on film.

Find occasions to force your child to think ahead. "You can only have one cookie today. Do you want it now or do you think you might enjoy it more after your bath?" "If I am late picking you up from nursery school, what will you do?" Think about the kinds of things you will be doing at Ginny's house, and then we can talk about the clothes you will need to pack."

When your child is learning to identify shapes, make a game of finding them around the house: a square picture frame, a round clock face, a triangular clothes hanger.

A trip to the supermarket is an education in itself, and it can be even more valuable to the preschooler who helps his parent plan ahead for the excursion. Let your child participate in the preparation of a shopping list. When you get to the store, he can help make decisions about purchases, learning to consider factors like need, size, or nutritional value. He can increase his vocabulary and learn to make comparisons. He can keep track of a few coupons, matching the words on a coupon with those on the corresponding product. And he can learn from you the importance of being a discriminating buyer.

A gift idea for a gifted child: purchase an inexpensive attaché case and fill it with a variety of arts and crafts materials.

paste	cotton balls
graph paper	a box of gummed stars
scissors	pieces of fabric
yarn	a paper punch
crayons	pencils
colored paper	a ruler
adding machine tape	colored chalk
popsicle sticks	pipe cleaners

Matching is easier than differentiating. When you are looking at and comparing leaves, seashells, or whatever, encourage your child to notice identifying properties. You can increase his understanding by arranging the materials so the similarities and the differences are apparent.

Do you remember how to make a toy parachute? All you need is a large handkerchief, some thread, and an empty spool for a weight.

Let your preschooler take an active part in the planning of your next trip. Decisions must be made about where to go, how long to stay, what to see and do, and so on. He can make a contribution. Let him.

If you can make a simple map showing the destination and some points of interest along the way, he can look at it before the trip and follow it as you go along. He will even learn to identify certain common map symbols.

A chalkboard can be perfect: for drawing pictures, practicing writing skills, and as a place to leave messages. Best of all, mistakes can be erased!

Ask questions that will make your preschooler look and listen. "What's making that strange noise I hear?" "Can you tell who is the birthday child in this picture?" "Which tree do you think this leaf fell from?" "Does it sound as if that ambulance is coming up our street?"

A big roll of butcher's wrap can be used for numerous artistic endeavors. A sheet can be torn off to protect a surface from wandering scribbles or paint splatters. A nice large piece can be cut from the roll to become the background for a holiday mural. Smaller pieces can be used for story writing or recording interesting events and, of course, for related illustrations.

A room (or space) of his own will help your gifted preschooler develop his independence, when he is responsible for picking up his own clothes and arranging his own possessions. Children also need a place to make a mess sometimes, to be able to keep projects without fear of losing them, to display their interests, and where, occasionally, they can just be alone.

Making predictions is a valuable skill. Testing them is too. Give your child experience in both: At bath time, "Which toy do you think will float?" When painting, "What will happen when you mix yellow and blue?" When cooking, "Would chocolate or butter frosting be better on this?"

Take time to explore an antique shop with your child. You may find samples of art, not only paintings, but on dishes and in the workmanship of fine furniture and jewelry. Many times the proprietor of a shop has fascinating tales to tell linking the past to old tables, kitchen equipment, maps, and the like.

Make a time line. Time lines are like yardsticks that measure events in time rather than distances. They can be as long and as inclusive as you want, but your preschooler's first exposure should be limited to no more than a few days. Later, longer periods of time can be used.

Draw a horizontal line on a strip of paper and along the line mark off divisions of time. Label the marks with pictures representing events in your child's life in the order they happen. For example, one day could begin with a picture of the sun, followed by a cereal bowl, then a swing set, a sandwich, a bed, a car, the Golden Arches, a bathtub, the moon, and finally, another bed.

A longer time line could show the relationships in time among family birthdays, holidays, and other important occasions.

Provide your child with plenty of opportunities to fit, stack, match, and compare; to count, learn nursery rhymes and songs, and label objects; to talk, listen, ask questions, and discover answers; to learn about physical principles and the difference between cause and effect; and to enjoy a variety of artistic and imaginative activities.

Most gifted children enjoy the challenge of a difficult, yet not impossible, task. For some preschoolers, the problem of arranging objects according to size fits this description. If yours can master this, let him try arranging pictures of various objects according to their actual size. Another challenging task is to arrange objects by their estimated weight and then, using a scale, to confirm the arrangement.

Give your child opportunities to improvise. The most valuable experiences are those where there is a real, rather than a contrived, need. When you run out of gift wrap, your preschooler can make some by decorating plain paper. If he needs shelves to display a collection, let him make his own out of cardboard boxes. An old spoon can do the job of a shovel. A worn sheet can be a tent, a cape, or a curtain for a stage.

Raise questions as you go about your daily routine: "How can we . . . ?" "Do you think that . . . ?" "Would it make a difference if . . . ?" "How many do you think . . . ?" "I wonder what would happen if . . . ?"

Take time to explain why you do certain things the way you do. "I'll put this letter by the door so I won't forget to mail it." "If I turn the handle of this pot toward the wall, no one will bump into it and spill the hot soup."

Children learn problem-solving techniques by solving problems. They learn to think of different ways of using things, or of approaching problems, by doing so when it needs to be done in real-life situations. Do not rob your child of the opportunities when they arise. But do not make the mistake of giving a young child an option when there really is none. A preschooler cannot decide when it is time to leave the playground, or how much to spend on a new outfit, or when he is old enough to play with matches!

Gifted children do not just collect: they gather, classify, study, and display. They pursue hobbies with an intensity that forces them to learn more than most of us realize there is to learn. This is all for a purpose: The more they learn, the more they will see and the more they see, the more they will learn. You will sometimes think your child's interests will take up all the space in the house, but it is worth it.

As your gifted child matures you want him to become aware that he can learn something from every situation, from everyone. Boredom **can** be avoided, because it comes from within. Teach him to take advantage of all types of opportunities from learning. Encourage self-initiated learning so he will have the ability to learn even in an unstimulating environment.

As you watch this little being develop into a thinking, questioning individual, thirsty for more knowledge, driven to new experiences, you will find yourself amazed by his ability to do things with these facts and experiences, sometimes even beyond your greatest expectations.

While he is a preschooler, you exercise most of the control over your child and are largely able to order the world in which his abilities and talents unfold. You try to be careful to see that he has the opportunity to develop physically, socially, emotionally, as well as cognitively.

But eventually you must send him off to a new environment, to school. The time of transition between the home and school and the kinds of programs offered for the preschooler and, later, for the gifted scholar are dealt with in Chapters 10 and 11. They provide information that can help you make several important decisions regarding your growing child.

10

The Preschool Experience

The age most children enter first grade is generally prescribed by state statute, usually around six. But the age a child first leaves his home to join other youngsters in a group or school-like environment varies greatly, often depending on chance, family work schedule or financial circumstances, and/or societal pressure rather than on the child's individual needs and his developmental stage. Because the kind of care a child receives during the first few years has such an impact on his total development, the decisions to put him in another's care, when to begin, and what kind of care should not be made lightly.

HOME CARE

Generally, a child under two and a half to three years old is better cared for in his home by his parent or parent substitute.

During the first few years, the child's learning is essentially egocentric. He is learning about himself and the world around him, about the laws of nature, through his senses, through trial and error, through repetition. If a certain action always gets the same reaction he learns about the constancy of the world; he learns trust. His self-concept is developing. If he feels loved, he develops a sense of self-worth. If his needs are met, he learns that he is important and capable of controlling his environment.

Few children under two and a half need more than an occasional playmate; most are not ready for the give and take required in a group of peers. But **every** young child needs a model (generally a caring adult) through whom he learns most of the elementary human behaviors.

A child models his developing speech patterns on those around him, particularly in the one-to-one interactions between caretaker and child. The way he will deal with other persons in the future is determined by the kind of relationship he has with his nurturer, as he will pattern much of his behavior on that of his model.

During most of his first three years, education is a natural process by which a child learns from a variety of experiences in which he acts upon his environment, teaching himself. There is no need at this time for direct instruction (such as we expect from a classroom teacher); rather, the role of the parent-educator is essentially one of providing opportunities for many varied sensory experiences, acting as a model, and interacting with the child as an individual. **The quality of these early interpersonal relations seem to have a lasting impact on the child's acquisition of many of the attitudes necessary to benefit from later formal instruction.**

Some parents believe their gifted toddlers need more freedom, flexibility, and stimulation than would be practical in a group situation and make temporary schedule adjustments so one of them can be at home during the child's waking hours. If the parent is unable or unwilling to provide this nurturing in the home, then substitute care could be considered: a grandparent, a neighbor, or a friend. Because the influence of a parent substitute is so strong, great care should be used in selecting one for a young child.

DAY CARE

The role of the day-care center has traditionally been one of custodial care, to serve the needs of the parent rather than the child. **Full-time enrollment is unlikely to be as beneficial to your gifted child's intellectual development as time spent in his own home during the first three years.** However, if the decision has been made to make use of day care for any portion of your child's day, you will want to insure that he receives the best care available under the circumstances. Since day-care centers are largely unregulated and tend to employ undertrained staff, it would be prudent to inspect the facilities carefully and speak with the personnel, establishing a good working relationship with each of the adults who will be directly involved with the care of your child.

In 1971, in response to the growing use of day-care centers the U.S. Department of Health, Education, and Welfare published a list of the necessities that the environment must provide to assure quality infant care. Use this list to insure that your child gets at least the necessities. And, as you read this condensed version of those guidelines, notice the emphasis on close, positive adult-child relationships.

1. Adequate nourishment.

2. Physical safety and relative comfort.

3. A relatively small number of adults having continuing, focused, and caring personal relationships with the child.

4. Frequent contacts with adults that are predominantly gratifying, expressive, and warm.

5. A "speaking partner" (verbal exchanges are essential).

6. The support of an adult who helps the child learn controls, to become competent and effective himself.

7. Adults who are examples of relative success, who are models for the child to imitate, and with whom he forms positive identifications.

8. Adults who respect the child as an individual.

9. Adults who are sensitive to, and respect, each child's different style of development and his uniqueness.

10. Activities must be organized around an acceptance of differences in tempo, style, and approach.Relative consistency, regularity, and order in the physical and interpersonal situation; stability of adults involved with the child.

11. Variety, flexibility, and change in the physical environment, within the structure of continuity.

12. Responses that are dependent on, and directly related to, the child's behavior.

13. Learning conditions conducive to the acquiring and practicing of skills; opportunities for action, and objects to manipulate, explore, and master.

14. Protection from overwhelming emotional states; freedom to express feelings and attitudes.

15. The sense of more gratification than frustration.

16. Freedom to be interested in, challenged by, and curious about what goes on around him.

17. Opportunities to develop socially and emotionally in an environment rich enough in appropriate stimuli to serve as a foundation for the development, expansion, and extension of thought process.

18. Adults who allow and expect a child to contribute according to his capacities

PLAY GROUPS

The neighborhood play group is an attractive alternative to constant home care. Parents of gifted toddlers often require a break and make arrangements with other parents to share duties for portions of the day. The children need not be of the same age but the number of children should be kept to a minimum (two to four youngsters in the group).

The cautious use of the play group can be satisfactory solution to child care problems. The advantages should be weighed against the disadvantages. You can choose an environment familiar to you, one that is nearby and has conditions similar to your home. But you must be realistic: some parents are not able to deal with groups successfully and many homes do not have room for more than one or two children.

If you can **find others who share your ideas about raising children,** who can give your child the kind of nurturing you want (and you can do the same for theirs), this situation can be an ideal one.

OTHER PROGRAMS

In many areas of the country new programs are being instituted for infant and toddler care, the focus being on the parent as an educator. The goal is to assist parents in developing effective parenting styles and to provide them with information on child development and certain activities to do with the infant to aid this development. There are several ways these programs can be worked. In some, the parent goes to a center to receive parenting instructions. In others, the child goes regularly to the center, with the parent going in at regular intervals to assist with the group of children. Or, a representative of the center makes home visits giving the parent help in any area that might have an effect on the child's development. A combination of these approaches can also be used.

NURSERY SCHOOL

When he is two and a half to three, your child may be ready to expand his horizons. You will notice that he is beginning to seek the companionship of other children. If he is sure and secure within himself and has developed a command of the language to such a degree that he is now more capable of the give-and-take demanded in a group setting, you might want to consider enrolling him in a nursery school.

A good nursery school, with a trained staff aware of the developmental patterns and needs of children this age, can offer some advantages not available in your home: more play space, a wide variety of appropriate equipment and materials, the companionship of other children, and contact with professionals.

There are some distinct disadvantages that must be considered. Children of three and four are still doing a major part of their learning through movement, through their senses and experimentation, driven by their curiosity and interests. **There is danger in overorganization.** Some nursery schools give the appearance of a good learning atmosphere while they actually stifle the very thing they purport to foster. Children of this age should be encouraged to choose their own activities whenever possible; not march to the tune of the teacher.

Choosing a good nursery school is not really all that difficult. Inspect the school yourself. Are the teachers warm, friendly, trained, perceptive? How many children are with each adult? Are the physical facilities clean, the rooms light and inviting? Is the playground fenced, the equipment well cared for? Is there space to run around? Are the materials, toys, and books appropriate for this age group and are they available for the children's use?

Talk to the director of the school. At this educational level, more than at any other, the atmosphere of the school is a reflection of the philosophy of the director. Does she realize that some three-year-olds are not ready to socialize, participate, and cooperate, and are provisions made for such children while they are being encouraged to develop these abilities? Is she aware of the need for a balance between over- and understimulation? Is the curriculum highly structured; are the youngsters given complete freedom; or is an attempt made to remain somewhere between these two extremes?

Ask if attendance can be scheduled to accommodate your child's maturity. Can the amount of school time—either the length of day or days per week—be modified? Can attendance be graduated as the child matures, from short periods a few days a week to longer periods more often?

Does the school encourage parent involvement? Does the staff understand the special needs of the gifted? Can you talk freely with them about your child's giftedness? Are they equipped to offer the challenges he needs? Do they realize that some bright children try to be like the other children, to please the teacher, by minimizing their abilities?

The nursery school experience may be the largest and most important step your child takes in the transition from home to school. It is usually a very beneficial, happy adventure for a gifted child, but **it is not an absolutely necessary one.** If your child does not go to nursery school, you should provide some corresponding opportunities for his growth: satisfactory peer contact, chances to be independent of parental presence and influence, the experience of being part of a group of three or more. This age is a good time to learn to accept the authority of adults other than the primary caretaker, in preparation for the time when a child begins his formal education.

If you do decide to send your child to a nursery school, it should be chosen with as much care as you used in providing a nourishing environment earlier. Consider not only your circumstances but also your child's needs.

KINDERGARTEN

Historically the nursery school has been oriented toward child development, whereas kindergartens have been school- and education-directed. Most public school systems offer kindergarten, but attendance is not always required. They are generally well housed, well equipped, and staffed with well-trained professionals.

The typical gifted child is ready, anxious, and eager to start school. This enthusiasm can sometimes lead to problems. Going there to learn, he takes with him some preconceived notions about all the exciting things he is going to be able to do. No one wants to disappoint a youngster this early in the game. You can save everyone involved considerable grief and assure your gifted child a meaningful educational experience from the very beginning simply through a little planning on your part.

Go to the school before the first day, preferably during the previous spring. Find out about the school and **by all means tell them about your child.** Don't worry about sounding boastful. You will be dealing with professionals who will appreciate pertinent information about a student. It would be unrealistic to expect the teacher—even the very best teacher —to realize immediately, without being forewarned, that your child already reads or has an understanding of math concepts far beyond that of the other children. Too many other problems demand attention in those hectic days when school begins.

The forewarned teacher can make preparations ahead of time for your child. The teacher who knows your child's capabilities can make sure his needs are being met from the first day of school. Get to know this teacher and set up a cooperative relationship early. While you should not expect your child's needs to receive a disproportionate share of teacher time and effort, you will be dealing with a professional whose job is to educate **all** the students, even yours.

Although the climate in the classroom and the direct instruction of the students are in the hands of the classroom teacher, the approach used often depends upon the school's view of child development and learning. These theoretical views of child development can fall anywhere along a continuum from "leave them alone, they'll mature naturally" to "they'll only grow if we intervene." The following brief descriptions of several of the prominent views will help you interpret the classroom activities and teacher techniques you encounter by improving your understanding of the philosophies behind them.

1. The **environmentalists'** view is that individuals are constantly influenced by forces in their environment. The teacher initiates the activities, which are chosen for their level of difficulty. Learning activities are viewed as self-rewarding.

2. The **behaviorists** define learning as a change in behavior. They make systematic use of positive reinforcements, approval of desired behavior.

3. **The developmentalists or maturationists** focus on the regularities within the organism. The child is allowed to set the pace in a loosely constructed, supportive environment. Activities are "matched" to the child's stage of development.

4. **Interactionists** assume development, learning, and behavior are substantially influenced by both the maturational process and environmental factors. This classroom tends to be highly structured because of the belief that the child does not develop while you wait.

5. The philosophy underlying the **open classroom** concept is belief in the value of spontaneity flowing from a child's interests. The student selects the activities in a classroom characterized by flexibility, pupil interaction, and a supportive rather than directive teacher.

One of these approaches is not necessarily better than the others. If the ultimate objective of a kindergarten program is to prepare the child for his years of formal education, it should generate students who want to learn, who are able to do it in a group situation, and who have the skills necessary to be academically successful.

Parents who want to observe how a kindergarten program functions should visit the school at midmorning, when the program is in full swing. If you cannot figure out what is going on, **ask.** "What are your goals and how do you accomplish them? Why are you doing this? Why aren't you doing something else?"

A note of caution

New preschools and child care centers are springing up all across our country. It has become a big business serving the estimated ten to eleven million children under the age of six. With not much more required of them than a room, a sign, and a health permit, it behooves parents to investigate thoroughly the people in whose care they place their preschool child. Caution is warranted. It is up to you to make an informed decision about how early you want your child to start school and what kind of environment would be best. There are many excellent preschools; find one of them.

GETTING READY

Your child's success in grade school and later will be largely determined by certain attitudes, skills, and abilities he brings with him. Whatever your decision regarding the kinds of preschool experiences your child has, you want to be sure he enters first grade with the basic skills necessary to benefit from formal group instruction.

Is Your Child Ready?

Many parents and preschool teachers are inclined to over-emphasize the importance of learning to count and to say the ABC's as indicators of later success in school. These skills are, of course, important . . . and fun . . . and measurable. But they are not as critical to school success as some other skills. Go through the following checklist to see how ready your child is for the demands that will be put on him in a classroom learning environment. Do this several months **before** he is scheduled to enter first grade so there will be time to work on any particularly weak areas.

If you discover more than you feel you can deal with successfully before the beginning of school, seek help. The school principal will be able to spell out the options available and offer sound professional advice. Make an appointment. Take enough pertinent information with you to the meeting to help you make a wise decision. A copy of the filled-out checklist would be helpful, as would evidence of your child's ability: some artwork or a project he has worked on; if he can read, take one or two books he can read easily; a sample of his writing; a note from his kindergarten teacher; and bring along any test scores you might have (IQ, readiness, achievement). The principal of a school is concerned that all students get off to a good start. Given enough time and information, the two of you, working together, can decide the best course for your child.

SCHOOL READINESS CHECKLIST

My child:

_____ has self-control: the ability to sit still, wait his/her turn, curb his/her impulses.

_____ can communicate well enough to make himself/herself understood.

_____ is able to understand and follow simple directions.

_____ can accept the authority of someone other than me.

_____ is able to function as a member of a group.

_____ feels secure away from familiar surroundings.

_____ will accept responsibility for his/her actions.

_____ can accept constructive criticism.

_____ is able to complete tasks without constant prodding.

_____ can see the connection between effort and accomplishment.

_____ is able to get started on a project without dawdling or wasting time.

_____ is able to resolve minor conflicts with peers.

_____ can attend to job at hand without being distracted by background noises.

_____ is able to do things for himself/herself, can work independently.

_____ will ask for help when he/she needs it.

_____ is able to make choices and accept mistakes.

_____ undertands that pictures and print represent real objects and ideas.

_____ strives to get things right but is not upset by every imperfection.

_____ has developed small muscle control—uses a pencil or scissors effectively.

_____ can continue working after minor interruptions.

_____ is not unduly influenced by another's approval or disapproval.

_____ likes to learn.

11

Your Child's Formal Education

While your gifted child is still preschool age, it is not too early to look into the kinds of programs that will be available to him when he enters the formal educational system. This chapter gives you an overall picture of typical programs designed for gifted students. With this knowledge, it is hoped you will be better equipped to prepare your child for that which lies ahead and to make wise decisions concerning his education.

The brighter your child is, the greater his need for special consideration. Some very good programs are offered in many public schools. It will be worth the effort to do a little investigating now, while there is still time either to join other parents of gifted children to push for special programs where none exist or to relocate to an area where they do exist.

PROGRAMS FOR THE GIFTED

Although the educational needs of gifted students are being met in a variety of ways, programs for the gifted can generally be classified into three basic types: enrichment, acceleration, and grouping.

Enrichment

Enrichment is perhaps the most widely used approach to the education of the gifted. In an enrichment program, the student is kept with his age peers while being given additional and in-depth studies to supplement the regular classroom curriculum. In some cases the enrichment focuses on activities—unrelated but in addition to the regular curriculum—deemed appropriate for the gifted child's cognitive or creative needs. These studies could take place within the regular classroom setting or be offered after school, on weekends, or during the summer months.

Ideally an enrichment program is planned to develop further the intellectual skills of the gifted child. It is meant to stimulate productive thinking and evaluation skills. Rather than meaning more of the same, it often means less. Because this child is gifted, it does not follow that he has more time than the other students. Frequently, due to out-of-school commitments, the gifted have less time than their peers. So, in a successful enrichment program, **special work is distinguished from additional work.** It can add depth to the learning experiences, allow the gifted student to remain with peers of the same physical and social ability, and it can foster the development of the child's leadership abilities.

The manner in which enrichment is handled in the classroom is usually decided by the individual teacher. Skilled techers, who are aware of the thinking processes of gifted children, can deal effectively with many of their needs through a variety of techniques. A primary teacher might ask the class to identify moving objects, while requiring the gifted child to order the moving objects from slowest to fastest. A third-grade class might be learning the multiplication tables and be given an assignment to do twenty problems. This assignment could then be tailored to the gifted students who would do only as many problems as necessary to show the teacher they understand. Then, they might be given some word problems requiring the use of the facts, or they might be told to make up some questions involving multiplication.

When a gifted student finishes a reading assignment before the regular classroom teacher even gets it out of her mouth, he might be allowed, or encouraged, to write an original play for the class to present, or use the extra time to complete a science display related to the science curriculum. In this case, enrichment is not interpreted to mean that the child simply read longer or more than the other students. Rather, he is asked to do something consistent with his special ability.

Another teacher might simply ask more complex questions of the gifted child—ones requiring higher thought processes than she asks of the classmates. Instead of asking the gifted child to name the twenty-second president of the United States, for example, this teacher might have him compare the executive powers of the twenty-second president with those of today's chief executive.

Another way of handling an enrichment program is to build on the individual's interests by initiating an independent project. Though directed by his regular teacher, the project may be unrelated to the standard classroom work. This might involve participation in a science fair, the publication of a newspaper, a report to the class, or something solely for his own intellectual satisfaction.

The rise of individualized instruction has been a contributing factor in the success of classroom enrichment programs. When all children are receiving instruction aimed at their individual level, the social cleavages often caused by one or two gifted students receiving special treatment are less likely to occur.

A good enrichment program often calls for more than even the most able classroom teacher is equipped to handle. There is first the problem of identification: it takes a trained professional to identify the gifted. It is not easy, since the most highly gifted—those in the greatest need of special help—are often the most difficult to spot.

We cannot make assumptions about the giftedness of a child based solely on the quality of his school work. The natural tendency is to mistake academic talent for giftedness. Good students are a delight to have in the classroom, but many times the behavior of the gifted child is less than delightful. He can be a disturbing element in the room. By the same token, the reverse is not always true. A parent or teacher may not assume the disruptive child is that way because he is gifted. It takes a professional, an expert, to tell the difference.

The back-to-basics movement put certain demands on the teacher who must be responding to the needs of the other twenty-eight students in the classroom. And the teacher who is aware of materials or an approcah appropriate for use with the gifted will also be aware that their use might be inappropriate in the regular classroom. One technique used successfully is to explore many areas with all the students, help them with the necessary, basic skills, then challenge the gifted to proceed on their own with in-depth studies. All of these approaches take time—time that the teacher just might not have.

In keeping the gifted at the learning level of his age peers, there is the danger that he will develop an unreal sense of what he can actually do or a sense of superiority because of the ease with which he attains excellence. The results can be the formation of poor work habits, an expectation of an effortless existence, boredom, or disruptive behavior. Special treatment for the one or two gifted in the room could also make them feel even more different or create feelings of jealousy on the part of the other children.

Many school districts restrict their enrichment offerings to weekends, vacation time, or after school. In practice, these programs are available to the most highly motivated, achieving students. Enrichment that takes place after school is preferable to no enrichment at all; however, it does not solve the problem of what to do with the gifted in the classroom. Fortunately, there are excellent teachers who are able to deal effectively with these problems and who find the experience exhilarating and challenging.

On last word about enrichment. Some parents have been able to offer their children their own enrichment program and have successfully prepared them to make the necessary personal adjustments to do well in the regular classroom with their age peers.

Acceleration

Acceleration is probably the oldest method we have used to meet the educational needs of our gifted students. It is designed to move the child into more advanced work earlier than his age group, and can be accomplished in a number of ways: grade skipping, early admission, or more rapid progress through the educational sequence.

Grade Skipping

Skipping grades was the accepted way of coping with the gifted for years. The justification for this practice was found in the original method of obtaining IQ: a mathematical equation in which the IQ equaled the mental age divided by the chronological age, multiplied by 100. Thus a four-year-old, whose performance on an intelligence test was the same as an average six-year-old, was said to have an IQ of 150. A ten-year-old with an IQ of 150 was said to have the mental ability of an average fifteen-year-old—was believed to think the same way as the average child five years his senior.

We know better. A ten-year-old with an IQ of 150 is not just a miniature fifteen-year-old. **He is a very bright youngster who thinks differently from average individuals of any age.**

Educators and parents observed that bright children tended to seek the companionship of older children and adults. Then, because of the ease with which the intellectually gifted child learned the materials presented to his age group, we assumed he would best function with older children whose chronological age matched his mental age. And, to a certain extent, this assumption proved to be true.

In practice, however, problems began developing. Some students were skipped along until they came to the point at which the subject matter or grade-level materials became too difficult for them. Then everyone would smile and say, "We finally found his level." A few, though, found grounds to question this conclusion. Had the accelerated student actually reached his limits, or had he missed some fundamentals needed to perform at or above this level?

A gifted child can have a problem with feeling different, and this feeling can be compounded if he is placed **too** far out of his age group. He is not only different intellectually, but among older children is probably different emotionally, physically, and socially as well.

The key problem in grade skipping, as with any program for the gifted, still remains to be faced: what to include in the program. Too often the methods of instruction and the depth of presentation are the same regardless of the grade level. The fact that the gifted student learns and thinks differently from all normal persons, no matter what the age, must be taken into consideration.

Early Admission

Another sort of acceleration is called early admission. Early admission can take place at different times in a child's educational career: kindergarten, first grade, or college.

The strict age requirements for entrance to kindergarten or first grade are not sacred; they are for the convenience of the school authorities. There is a wide range of intellectual abilities among five-and six-year-olds. A gifted child who is mature physically and socially will usually benefit from early admission to kindergarten or first grade. It seems to be to their advantage if they are within one year of the normal entrance age. At the other end of the educational ladder, some universities offer early admission to outstanding high school students.

In many high schools the course offerings for the final year are limited and usually the gifted student has already met most of the requirements for graduation. Rather than just coasting through, or wasting this year, the solution for some seniors is take courses for university credit while remaining with their age peers in school.

Instead of entering college at a young age, a student can finish high school, then move directly into the sophomore or higher level by taking a proficiency test. During their senior year, students can take the College-Level Examination Program (CLEP) tests and earn college-level credit for knowledge or proficiency in certain areas, as measured by performance on the test. Many parents prefer this method of early entrance for financial reasons. The student could conceivably earn one year's tuition for the price of one day's testing. The student is then able to get immediately into the meat of his college career, skipping those sometimes dreary freshman courses.

Rapid Progression

A third approach to acceleration is through more rapid progression through the educational sequence via the ungraded primary, two grades in one, advanced placement, extra courses, and credit by examination.

In an ungraded primary the content for the traditional three grades is offered in a continuing block called the primary. The child can progress through this primary block at his own rate, making it possible for a student to enter the fourth grade after as little as two years. Other students may take four years to complete this primary progression, but all remain close to their chronological peers. While some exceptional pupils could do the work in only one year, they are usually required to take two, giving them the extra time to develop socially, to delve into the curriculum in greater depth, while providing them opportunities to develop leadership skills with their near-age peers.

Some schools put two grades together. In these combination classes, the gifted student can be allowed to complete two grades in one year thereby reducing the likelihood of missing basic concepts and keeping him near his age group. The gifted student may go on to the next grade with half of the class, cutting one year off his schooling with relative ease.

Advanced placement, extra courses, and credit by examination are techniques commonly used at the high school and college levels. A bright student could take one or more extra courses each semester, thus advancing his graduation date by as much as a year.

The parents of the **extremely** gifted child will have more decisions to make because acceleration is always considered for **this** child, no matter what kind of gifted program the school offers. The decision on how far to accelerate must be made on an individual basis, with the advice of a professional. There have been many instances in which the very young have been successfully accelerated up to the university level. Usually, the parents of such a child have worked hard with him for years to develop a good self-concept as well as the social skills needed to interact with both chronological and intellectual peers. They have also seen that he was able to form satisfactory close personal relationships.

Other parents of the highly gifted have rejected extreme acceleration, choosing instead to keep their child within a few years of his age group. But it has been necessary for them to see that their child's cognitive needs were met in the hours after school.

Through acceleration, gifted pupils are allowed to advance academically at a faster pace, giving them a chance at an early start on their productive years. Additionally, fewer years in school mean less expense all the way around. The disadvantages of a program of acceleration include these possibilities: serious learning gaps could develop; there might be a little time for the bright student to reflect upon and explore general concepts; and it could compound the exceptional child's feelings of differentness as well as reduce his chances of developing his leadership skills. There always remains the question of what to include in the program. The gifted are capable of moving in directions that another higher grade level might not provide any more than his present grade. However, many of the shortcomings of this type of program can be lessened by accelerating groups instead of individuals.

Grouping

Some schools devise various ways of grouping students to provide for the educational needs of the gifted. This grouping can take place for all, or part, of the school day in the regular classroom, in special classes within the student's school, or the gifted are sometimes grouped in a separate, specialized facility.

The greatest advantage of grouping is that the curriculum can be tailored to the gifted students' peculiar educational needs. For the highly gifted, there is a special value. Educators have found that the nature of the group he is in tends to influence the social adjustment of the highly gifted and, in situations in which he does not differ markedly from the average ability of the group, he is more able to form compatible relationships.

Within the Classroom

A teacher with a heterogeneous group in a self-contained classroom typically divides the class into subgroups for instructional purposes. Whatever they are called—bluebirds, redbirds, or yellowbirds—the class is divided into ability groups: the good students, the poor students, and the others. This type of grouping can work if it is handled very skillfully so the self-concept of each group is protected. The low group must not feel inferior, nor should the high group get an unrealistic impression of the value of academic superiority.

Although many primary teachers group only for reading and math, and the same pupils tend to be in the same group for both, the grouping can be rearranged during other parts of the day so each child learns that he is "good" at something the teacher values.

The high group must learn that high achievement is not reached without effort. The teacher should plan a different curriculum for them, not one that merely means going through the book faster or doing more math problems than the rest of the class, but one utilizing activities that tap their higher cognitive processes.

Pull-out Grouping

The gifted can also be served on a part-time basis within the school by pulling them out of the regular program for specialized instruction, utilizing an itinerant teacher and/or a resource room. The itinerant teacher, one who is specially trained in meeting the needs of the gifted, moves from room to room, or school to school, teaching selected students for a certain number of hours per day or week. The resource room, usually with a directing teacher, can also serve the gifted child's needs. It might be housed in a section of the library or it could even be an elaborately equipped learning center. Its function can be merely to provide a retreat to share thoughts or to read alone, or it can be a hive of creative activity, depending upon the students' needs and the school's resources.

In the upper grades, grouping of the brighter students can be accomplished by means of honors programs, seminars, special courses, or multitrack programs. Some schools sponsor clubs or teams for those children who display special aptitude in various academic areas. You can even find private camps and publicly sponsored summer programs for gifted children.

In some locations, programs of independent study are built around the interests of the student. A few schools offer a mentor program to the more able students. The mentor is generally a member of the community who has a special skill or interest who does not merely disseminate information but allows the student to observe him in his work and interacts with him on a personal level.

Separate Facilities

Occasionally a school district will set aside an entire campus for the gifted within the area. This practice is exceedingly rare. The classes, teacher, and students are pulled together into one environmental setting and the total curriculum is structured on the learning characteristics of the gifted student. The teachers are chosen for their ability to work with these children and resource persons are readily available for use by faculty or students alike. When the gifted are grouped in this way, opportunity exists for interaction among children of varying ages.

In the total school setting allowances can be made for creative behavior, individuality, and the student's need for more self-direction, without unsettling the instructional routine of the average student. This kind of solution can be very demanding on the teachers: it is not an easy job, for they must expect to give more in the way of time and energy, both intellectually and physically. It does, however, grant the teacher the latitude to introduce materials and to conduct class in ways that might be inappropriate in the typical classroom.

However children are grouped, the results are not consistently higher when you narrow the ability range without constructively altering the programs for the various levels.

When the gifted students are grouped, they must put forth more effort to achieve excellence within the group, motivating them to work harder in an atmosphere that is usually more stimulating. There is increased possibility of establishing harmonious relationships with other children and less fear of rejection. The gifted seem to be more creative and more modest in a homogeneous group where they are not so different and where they learn there are many others of equal or greater ability. For some children, though, the concern for achievement and the competition in this type of a setting may be too pressing.

The private school alternative

Many parents exercise the option of sending their children to private schools. Such schools may offer a particular educational emphasis, religious orientation, or apparent social and cultural benefits. Whatever the attraction of any given private institution, parents of gifted children must be sure to subject that school to the same criteria used to evaluate public schools. All the standards and qualities demanded of public school programs for the gifted should be looked for when you consider the private school alternative. That a school is private rather than public is no automatic guarantee that is the best place for your gifted child to be educated.

WHAT TO LOOK FOR IN A GIFTED PROGRAM

Parents must sometimes be persistent in finding the right program for their gifted child. It is important enough to your child and to your investment in his education to take the time to look over the situation carefully by going to the school and observing what is going on, talking to the teachers and the students, and referring to the following checklist to guide you in your observation.

This list is intended to give you something to look for other than a large library, or a beautiful science laboratory (which are certainly nice to have but not critical). A good gifted program will incorporate most of the items on this checklist.

CHECKLIST FOR GIFTED PROGRAMS

____ Do the students appear to be eager for knowledge and know how to find it?

____ Is there evidence of self-expressive activities such as art, drama, or dance?

____ Do the teachers seem to be using a variety of instructional practices?

____ Would this atmosphere foster originality and creativity?

____ Is time allowed for the students to interact among themselves and with the faculty?

____ Is it obvious that the curriculum has sequence and direction?

____ Are the teachers able to explain the purpose of classroom activities and instructional practices?

____ Is there a degree of flexibility in the rules and procedures?

____ Does the staff recognize the wide range of abilities in gifted children?

____ Is the climate a supportive and accepting one in which limits are clearly set?

____ Are the students required to evaluate not only the results of an undertaking but the process used as well?

____ Are the students strong in both the basic and research skills?

_____ Are there opportunities for the students to develop leadership skills?

_____ Are the students required to use higher cognitive levels of analysis, synthesis, and evaluation, rather than just working at higher grade levels?

_____ Is there an emphasis on productive thinking?

_____ Are the students encouraged to evaluate facts and arguments critically?

_____ Are there opportunities to excel and receive recognition for achievement?

_____ Are the students given freedom to make educational decisions?

_____ Are the students free to consider controversial issues?

_____ Are there problem-solving opportunities germane to the students' lives?

_____ Are the students held responsible for their actions?

_____ Are independent work and self-teaching encouraged?

_____ Is the atmosphere scholarly and challenging?

_____ Would this program be better for my child than what he is presently receiving?

WHAT TO LOOK FOR IN A TEACHER

Regardless of the kind of educational program a school offers the gifted student, its implementation relies on the talents of the teachers. Naturally, we all wish our children could have excellent teachers year after year, but not even the "perfect" teacher will be ideal for every student.

If you have seen that your child enters school with a strong personal and educational foundation, even several years of mediocre teaching will not hinder him. Sometimes a student needs only one great teacher to spark a flame that cannot be extinguished. You can hope that all your child's teachers like working with the gifted and demand that they do your child no harm.

While no test has been devised to predict who will be the ultimate teacher, those who are most successful with gifted students generally possess the following characteristics:

Intelligence

Common sense tells us that superior intellectual ability would be a desirable trait in a teacher of the gifted. Bright students prefer bright teachers who are able to communicate on higher abstract levels.

Flexibility

The teacher should have the ability to change established patterns and to reach beyond the established curriculum.

Creativity

Gifted children are predictable in their unpredictability, and teacher should be able to deal with the unexpected in creative ways, with imagination, and unusual approaches to classroom management.

Self-Confidence

Gifted students will challenge authority. Their teachers must be able to encourage questions and independence, accepting the role of a guide and a resource person rather than that of the authority. A secure and unthreatened personality is a must.

Knowledge

The teacher of the gifted must have an in-depth knowledge not only of his subject but, ideally, be possessed of a variety of interests. The teacher should have a clear understanding of the learning process and the learning characteristics of the gifted.

Sensitivity

A good teacher of the gifted is sensitive to the unique emotional/intellectual natures of these students.

Every child should have a teacher who understands his educational needs and learning characteristics; the gifted student is entitled to no less. His teacher must have a respect for and an interest in the gifted, with a willingness to learn from as well as teach them. A nature that is not satisfied with mediocre achievement, either in himself or in the students, is a desirable trait. Not all gifted children are the same, but the teacher should certainly be aware of the typical characteristics that influence their classroom behavior.

THE EDUCATIONAL CHARACTERISTICS OF GIFTED CHILDREN

The teacher of gifted children can expect to be working with students who are not only so many grade levels ahead of their peers, but who think differently from other children—faster and at higher levels of abstraction, complexity, and difficulty. They learn easily, and require less drill. Sometimes poor in spelling, careless in handwriting, and inaccurate in math, they are impatient with details that require rote learning. These independent workers can handle more things at one time than most students, and they require less supervision and direction. They see relationships and grasp ideas readily, learning rationally rather than by sheer memory. Generally observant, gifted children often perceive things others miss, seeing ahead to possible results that make them want to persist in a project when others might want to quit, or to quit when others want to persist.

Sometimes so quick to see an answer, without going through the routine steps, they tend to be lackadaisical in completing assignments. Bored by the slow pace and intellectual confinement of the standard curriculum, the gifted often respond by being troublemakers, disturbing those around them. They can be inattentive, restless, and demanding. Their insatiable curiosity prompts questions that differ in depth, scope, frequency, and type. They are dissatisfied with standard explanations.

The gifted have a wide range of interests with an unusual ability to generalize, resulting in a broad fund of information. Their large vocabularies are accompanied by exceptional verbal ability. Gifted children tend to be more interested than others in social and ethical problems. They choose to spend work and play time with mental peers—with their age peers they frequently feel so different that they may attempt to isolate themselves or act average. Although they can appear haughty and critical of others, their drive to excel and their self-imposed standards sometimes give them deep feelings of inferiority. They seem compelled to show others how to do things and do everything within their power to quicken the pace in the classroom.

They do not always make life easy for teachers. Their very presence can pose a threat to some.

Gifted children need expert help in fulfilling their potential. They must learn the importance of educating themselves and of the value of hard work. Their creative abilities must be constructively channeled. Capable of so many different kinds of success, they may have a problem confining themselves to a reasonable number of enterprises.

A special program implemented by specially trained teachers can capitalize on the educational characteristics of gifted students.

HOW TO GET YOUR CHILD INTO A SPECIAL PROGRAM

If, by the time your child reaches school age, you are convinced that he has exceptional abilities and his educational needs are not being met by the routine classroom instruction, perhaps you ought to investigate the possibility of getting him into a special program for the gifted. In many cases, admission to a gifted program comes after the child has been identified as intellectually superior through a routine screening of students (see Chapter 12). If your child has not been selected by the school as part of the regular screening process, there are several steps you can follow:

1. Keep records. Those children hardest to identify as gifted are usually the ones most in need of special help in the educational program and often the only clue to their giftedness comes from the parent. Your notes listing things you have observed about your child can aid the school in determining his special educational needs.

2. Ask questions. Find out what kind of a program is offered locally. Is it a good one? Would your child benefit from it? Ask how eligibility for admission is determined.

3. Seek help from authorities. The first person to contact would logically be your child's present teacher, or one from a previous year. If the teacher is unable or unwilling to help, see the principal. If individual testing is required, the school system may employ someone who routinely administers the tests and the principal might be able to arrange an appointment for your child. If this strategy fails, you might have to make arrangements on your own. You can contact a psychologist, your local mental health association, or the education or psychology department of a nearby university. (You might have to pay for this testing.) Then take the results to the superintendent of schools.

If all this fails and you are still unsuccessful, and if the test results confirm your beliefs that your child is gifted, you can contact one of the agencies listed in Chapter 5.

Do not be put off by this procedure. You have every right to see that your child's educational needs are being met.

HIGHER EDUCATION

Your gifted child should certainly attend college, and will probably go on to professional school or advanced graduate studies. Higher education is expensive and requires planning to become a reality for most. While we are seeing a trend to financial assistance for the intellectually able student, aid is often based on perceived financial need and is limited to a very few. The plums are offered to the very bright who give evidence of future achievement—those who show signs of leadership, ingenuity, perseverance—the student who can list more than just good grades on his transcript. It might be wise to start encouraging your child in these directions now.

The name of the school is not the sole factor to be considered when choosing a college or university. The general intellectual climate, the proportion of able and inspiring teachers, and the effort expended to discover and motivate the gifted are important. To think about choosing the university for your child at this time is probably just an exercise in futility. Being the freethinker he is, he will want to make his own decision when the time comes.

SUMMARY

Educators recognize that there are many and varied categories of giftedness and within each area there are degrees of exceptionality. It would be unreasonable to expect the schools to meet all the needs of all gifted children in all realms of physical, social, and mental development or in all areas of the creative arts. Most schools recognize the special needs of the highly gifted—but these children are so rare! Most schools attempt to meet some of the educational needs of gifted children in one way or another. Some are more successful than others.

We can expect the schools to try to attend to the intellectual needs of all students. When intellectual exceptionality requires treatment that cannot be provided in the traditional way, an attempt should be made to tailor a more suitable program.

The schools have a variety of ways of handling the gifted student. The success of these programs depends largely on the implementation by the teacher and to an even greater extent upon the preparation and attitude of the individual student.

It is your responsibility to prepare your child, to offer support and enrichment not only in the early years but throughout the school years as well. Parental responsibility does not end when the child enters school.

12

Testing the Gifted

Y ou suspect that your child may be gifted and are trying to do the best job of parenting, fulfilling his needs both as a child and as a gifted person. Parental caring is done out of love, a feeling of responsibility—without question. There will come a time, however, when he will have needs requiring special treatment that is not always given so freely by others. The availability of special help is often dependent upon proof of his unique ability, the empirical evidence provided by a test.

T-E-S-T, a four-letter word?

There is certainly no getting around the fact that we live in a test-oriented society. We must take a test before we can drive our cars, to determine if we can enter the college of our choice, even to prove we are qualified to remain employed in the field of our expertise. While we might have some doubts about the validity of some of these tests, we can usually see their purpose.

Are there good reasons to test cognitive ability? Certainly. A test of intellectual ability, properly administered **and** evaluated can be an invaluable tool for pinpointing strengths and weaknesses in abilities valued in our culture, abilities that can be more fully developed through proper nurturing. Furthermore, a test score can open doors to opportunities and valuable educational experiences. On the other hand, **indiscriminate testing done without a valid purpose should be avoided.**

Let us look at the kinds of tests commonly used to determine cognitive ability during infancy, the preschool years, and later in school. The more you know about these instruments and their uses, the better equipped you will be to see that they are used to help your child, to open doors.

INFANT TESTING

Only in rare instances do sufficient reasons exist for the formal testing of an infant—usually to detect some abnormality that appears to be interfering with normal developmental patterns. Almost without exception, the earlier problems are identified, the greater the chance for correcting or compensating for them. By and large, the so-called intelligence tests administered to the infant are heavily weighted on motor development and attention, and most experts agree that these tests have little value in predicting later higher mental functioning. **Usually the gifted child does not behave much differently from his average peers in these areas in the first few years.**

You know that children all go through spurts of growth. These peaks and valleys, periods of calm and disequilibrium, cause the results of any test given one week to differ substantially from those given a few weeks later. So, if testing is indicated, a series of tests will give a truer picture than a single testing.

The most widely used infant tests are the Gesell Developmental Scales, the Bayley Scales of Mental and Motor Development, and the Cattell Infant Intelligence Scale. The Gesell

Developmental Scales are a direct outgrowth of the extensive observations of the development of normal infants by Arnold Gesell and his associates who recorded behaviors in minute detail, classifying them into four domains: adaptive, motor, personal-social, and language. These behaviors were then ordered, progressing from the earliest simplest infant responses to the walking/talking problem-solving of the child in his second year and beyond.

Gesell saw intellectual growth as a matter of maturation, a process of development with deviations due to "superior endowments" or "environmental retardation." The Bayley and the Cattell Scales similarly record the infant's progress from simple perceptual motor task to the more complex manipulatory and verbal functions, with the assumption that the intellectual development of an infant is closely related to his motor development.

While these tests of infant ability can pick up signs of developmental lag, **they are not very successful in distinguishing the superior child from the total population** because intellectual achievement is affected by some other areas of development, which can and should be tested in early life.

Areas affecting intellectual development

The central nervous system (the brain and spinal cord) is the physical basis for all mental development. A physician has undoubtedly checked your child's neurological development by observing reflexive behaviors like sucking and the responses of the soles of the feet and the pupils. The importance of this examination cannot be overemphasized.

Most of your child's later learning will be through his two senses of sight and hearing. Their proper functioning can have a critical influence on his intellectual development. The word "functioning" is chosen purposefully. We are speaking here of more than just knowing if the infant is stone deaf or totally blind.

How well do his eyes work? Some optometrists are particularly interested in the way the eyes work together, testing three-dimensional vision, convergence, and tracking ability.

Problems in these areas can cause severe learning difficulties and would not be detected by the familiar eye chart test, nor by the inspection of the health of the eye. If caught early, a problem often can be remedied by simple exercises.

A hearing deficit can be more debilitating than a visual one, particularly when language is rapidly developing (six months to two years). It is not simply a matter of being able to hear sounds, but of being able to block out extraneous or background noise, as well as the ability to detect subtle differences in sounds. Hearing screenings that can pick up discrimination problems can be given as early as three and a half months. Ideally, all babies should have this aspect of their hearing tested. Certainly, if there is any question at all about the child's language development, it should be investigated.

While language and intellect are inextricably bound together, tests of language development are not very reliable in assessing the intellectual development of the very young. One reason is that most language ability, in infants, is receptive rather than spoken language. It is even difficult to determine the extent of a toddler's language development because much of what he can say requires interpretation by a parent. Additionally, a one and a half- to two-year-old is typically uncooperative in a testing situation.

Several tests or observational instruments applicable during the first few years have evolved out of the research of Swiss psychologist Jean Piaget. These tests, which relate to sensorimotor intelligence, are presently technically less well refined than those developed for older children, but they are nevertheless quite valuable in monitoring early intellectual growth.

If these infant tests have little predictive value, is there anything that has? Perhaps. According to several respected authorities, **general alertness in infants seems to correlate with later tests of intelligence.** Also, many studies have determined that **the parent's perception of a child's ability is generally more reliable than the tests.** For the most part, all tests of intellectual ability become more reliable and more predictive as the child matures.

TESTING THE PRESCHOOLER

Sometime around the end of the second year, or beginning of the third, parents become aware of the emergence of thinking ability as evidenced in their child's use of language. This little being has suddenly, it seems, left infancy behind. Intelligence testing at this age becomes more meaningful than that done during infancy.

There are numerous tests on the market specifically designed for use with the preschooler. The particular instrument used should be selected **and** administered by an expert —someone familiar with the test and its limitations. (Those do-it-yourself kits on the market today are absolutely worthless!) Several of the preschool tests have been found to be moderately successful in predicting later intelligence test performance. The most well-known and respected instruments used at this age bear the names of two giants in the field: Binet and Wechsler.

The Stanford-Binet can be used with a child as young as two—provided the child is cooperative. The test is based on the assumption that the average child can do more and more complicated tasks better each year. For instance, an average five-year-old can copy a square but not a diamond. A four-year-old can repeat three digits, a seven-year-old can repeat five.

The Wechsler Preschool and Primary Scale of Intelligence (WPPSI) is intended for the four- to six and a half-year-old child. Wechsler contended that the important difference between his test and others was his "metric of moreness or lessness" rather than the presence or absence of correct answers.

You may have noticed, during the course of a regular checkup, your pediatrician has asked your preschooler to do some things, and wondered why. A child's ability or inability to stand on one foot, to copy a circle, square, triangle, or diamond, to look through a pinhole in a sheet of paper, can all give the doctor a rough estimate of the child's intellectual development. These tasks might be considered an IQ test of sorts.

How to get your preschooler tested

If you believe it is in your child's best interest to have an intelligence test, the first thing to do is gather evidence to support your conviction that he may be gifted. Simply sit down and write a list of specific advanced behaviors and the ages at which they appeared. Take this list with you when you go to talk to people about testing your child.

Your first contact can be with your pediatrician or family physician. Ask to be referred to a psychologist who specializes in testing preschoolers. You might want to contact the local central school district office, a mental health association, or the family/child counseling services. Another possible route would be to communicate with the education or psychology departments of a nearby university. (You will probably have to bear the cost of the testing at this time; if you wait until your child is in school, the school usually pays for it.)

Keep trying, if you really think it is important enough. You might have to be very persistent. While most experts will agree that IQ testing of the preschooler is not generally recommended, all acknowledge the fact that in some individual cases (especially in regard to extreme giftedness or exceptionally great developmental deviations) the problems can be as great as those that go with mental retardation and should be attended to as early as possible. If you are still having trouble getting help, first review your "evidence," then contact one of the organizations listed in Chapter 5.

TESTING THE SCHOOL-AGE CHILD

You probably will not have to initiate the action to have your school-age child tested, because the schools are becoming increasingly aware of the special educational needs of the gifted and recognize the importance of early intervention. At the same time, they are becoming more expert at the identification of the gifted.

A word about the term "identification." When educators speak of the gifted in their schools, they speak of those who have been identified as gifted. The inference, of course, is that not all of the gifted students have been, or even can be, found. The identification procedures are by no means infallible. If you are convinced that your child is one of those who is gifted but has not been identified, you could follow the procedure outlined in Chapter 11 for getting a child into a special program. The usual procedure, though, is generally that of screening followed by testing.

Screening

Screening is that method by which the school gathers evidence to indicate the possibility that a child is gifted. It would certainly be impractical and unnecessary to test every child; on the other hand, to lessen the possiblity of missing someone, many different methods are used, singly or in combination, to find the students who might have exceptional potential. Some of the more commonly used are teacher observation, achievement test results, honor roll membership, special ability (math, art, leadership), creativity tests, behavior checklists, and parent recommendations; but the single most effective and efficient tool for screening is a group IQ test. **Unfortunately, it is also the most widely abused instrument of all.**

Group IQ tests

An IQ test given to a number of students at the same time is called a group IQ test. These tests are quite effective in identifying a large percentage of the gifted in a given group and are efficient in that most of the children identified are indeed gifted.

One of the greatest problems with group tests is their tendency to select the academically talented. This fault is the main reason the other means are used in the attempt to find the gifted child who is not doing as well in school as one would expect.

Children with exceptionally high IQs cannot be accurately picked up on a group test because these tests are designed to measure the whole spectrum of cognitive ability and, in order to tap the widest range, many of the questions are not appropriate for the highly gifted. Another difficulty in trying to measure the ability of the highly gifted is the fact that the ceiling (highest possible score) may be too low. This is true not only of group tests but of some individual tests as well. For instance, the highest possible score a fourteen-year-old can get on the Stanford-Binet is 167, the Wechsler is 154, the Otis Quick Scoring Test of Mental Ability (Beta) is 143, the California Test of Mental Maturity (Elementary) is 136, and the Lorge-Thorndike Intelligence Test (Verbal Battery) is 150. Obviously, the highest scores on these tests are exceptional, but some very gifted children will not be able to show their full superiority.

A general rule could be: **The closer the score is to the ceiling, the greater the odds that it is too low.** This reason is why many schools will use a lower cutoff point on a screening device than that which is suggested for inclusion in the gifted program.

A great discrepancy can exist between the IQ obtained on a group test and that revealed by an individual test. A child who scores 120 on a group test could conceivably score as high as 180 on an individual test. The child with an IQ of 180 is extremely different from the one with a 120 IQ, and this difference is important.

To compensate for some of these problems, the extremely gifted are often given a test designed for an older group. It is believed that their ability will be better measured by this technique.

Individual IQ tests

An individual IQ test is one which is designed to be administered by a trained person to one child at a time. The great advantage over group tests is that the test giver can observe and interpret the child's actions. If he appears to be too tense, or does not seem to understand what is required, adjustments may be made. Offbeat answers can be dealt with. If the questions are too hard or too easy, the level can be adjusted. A truer picture of ability can be seen because this tester can begin at the child's apparent level, thus increasing his interest and motivation. (Alfred Binet, the father of IQ testing, observed that the child will give up if the starting point is too difficult and will make no effort to do well if it is too simple.)

Individually administered IQ tests are expensive and time-consuming, but they have a long and respected history of recognized ability to test the extremes of intellectual functioning. While these tests do not measure **all** the important cognitive abilities, emphasizing those qualities that tend to make a successful student, they are designed to measure the child's potential in those areas traditionally held important in our culture. They focus on the abilities usually considered indicative of intellectual capacity: to reason, to define verbal concepts, to perceive essential similarities and differences, to relate past knowledge to present situations, to understand abstract concepts, and to respond to new situations.

Culture-fair tests

Questions are being asked about IQ tests. Are they culture-bound? Are they unfair to certain segments of society? Evidence is presented for both sides of the issue.

It is unlikely that any test can be completely culture-**free.** To a certain extent, the type of culture determines the value placed on certain abilities. Ours is a culture that values communication, reasoning, problem-solving, and other abstract abilities.

An attempt is being made to detect the presence of these abilities in a culturally **fair** type of test, one in which language, for example, would play a lesser role. Typical tasks might be the arrangement of form boards, completion of missing parts, and the assembling of discrete parts into wholes. One such test can even be administered in pantomime. The goal is to determine the intelligence of a person without penalty for his cultural background.

IQ TEST QUESTIONS

Different tests use different means to determine the extent of a child's cognitive ability. Some are timed; some are not. Not all answers are either right or wrong and sometimes more than one try is allowed for a task. Tests may be oral, or written, or a combination of the two. They can measure verbal and/or nonverbal performance, but they all require response to questions or the performance of specific tasks. The child's age and the instrument used determine exactly what will be involved.

The following is a list of the kinds of tasks typically included in some of the widely used IQ tests:

Name the objects in a picture.

Repeat a set of numbers.

Repeat sentences.

Compare objects.

Define words.

Solve problems using common sense or practical judgment.

Observe and/or explain similarities in two or more things.

Solve oral arithmetic problems.

Answer information questions.

Tell what is missing from a picture.

Put things into categories.

Work through a maze.

Follow directions.

Arrange a set of pictures in order.

Duplicate a block design.

Copy a pattern.

Select the drawing that does not belong in a set.

See a pattern in a series.

Count blocks in a stack in which some are hidden.

Associate numbers or shapes with specific symbols.

Put a puzzle together.

Give uses for things.

Give reasons for some common practices.

Find the hidden figure.

The following are examples of items that might be included on a written IQ test:

1. Mark the thing farthest from the box.

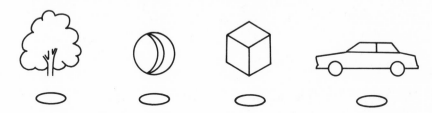

2. Mark the girl who is holding something with both hands and is not standing.

3. Find the drawing that belongs next in the series.

4. Which picture goes with the two pictures in the box?

5. Which number does not belong in the pattern made by the other four?

2   4   5   6   8

◯   ◯   ◯   ◯   ◯

6. Which two blocks are the same?

◯   ◯   ◯   ◯   ◯

7. Which word does not go with the others?

car   bicycle   football   airplane   train

◯   ◯   ◯   ◯   ◯

8. Ten is one-half of what? _____

9. Robin is to bird as trout is to _____.

big   line   fish   mother

◯   ◯   ◯   ◯

10. Find the picture that is hidden in this pattern.

◯   ◯   ◯

PREPARING YOUR CHILD FOR TESTING

As you can see, these questions are not the kinds you can sit down and teach your child just before he enters the test room. But it does stand to reason that there are certain things you can do for and with your gifted child, especially prior to an individual test, so his performance during the test will give a truer indication of his exceptional ability.

1. **Tell him why he is being tested.** If he is bright, you will not be able to fool him. Use your common sense; you know how he will react. You want to motivate him to do well, not scare him to death or put excessive pressure on him.

2. **Tell him what to expect.** Find out about the size of the room, whether it will be an oral or a written test, how long the test will last. You will want to prepare your child for this new experience. Just as you would not send him into a dental examination alone without any preparation, there is no need for secrecy about the setting for an IQ test. Introduce your child to the tester, and tell them where you will be during the testing session.

3. **Be sure your child can follow directions!**

4. **Be sure your child can relate to adults other than his parents.** You want him to perform as well for the tester as he would for you.

Who will do well on an IQ test?

Some children will do better on the test than others who are no less intelligent. Undoubtedly the better performance will be turned in by the child who has:

- had the opportunity to acquire information and build up his vocabulary.
- had the chance to use his common sense to reach solutions to problems in his everyday life.
- been exposed to basic arithmetic processes as they relate to his own experiences.
- an understanding of the concept of "sameness" and "difference."
- learned to pay attention and recall auditory information in proper sequence and detail (such as in storytelling).

- the ability to visualize essential from nonessential details.
- had opportunities to participate in social situations.
- developed the ability to synthesize parts into meaningful wholes.
- developed good visual-motor coordination.
- learned to question things he does not understand.

Although you would not want to teach your child a list of words and definitions as a way of cramming for an IQ test, you **can** build his vocabulary through everyday conversation, reading, and by taking him places. If your child has been accustomed to solving problems, making decisions, and looking for similarities and differences in things around him, he will certainly be better prepared to take this kind of a test.

The skills he needs to do well on an IQ test are not taught in a few days or weeks, but are developed over a period of years. With a little ingenuity on your part, most are easily slotted into your everyday interactions with your child.

INTERPRETING TEST RESULTS

IQ tests measure more than simple innate ability. A child's performance can be influenced by his reaction to the environment and even by his motivation at the time of the test. No test is perfect, but if there is a fault, it will more often involve the interpretation of the results than some intrinsic flaw in the test itself.

At the beginning of this chapter it was pointed out that tests must be properly administered and evaluated. An integral part of the evaluation process lies in the interpretation of the results—usually to the parent by the person who administered the test. Consequently, a basic knowledge of test "vocabulary" and the meaning of the different kinds of scores used will help you to understand this interpretation.

We are all familiar with the teacher-made tests. We took them as students and understood that an 88 meant that we got 88 percent of the answers correct and the score of 88 probably translated into a grade of "B." A "B" was GOOD. We knew other things too. A "B" from one teacher could mean something quite different from another teacher's "B." Sometimes the tests were fair, sometimes not. They might or might not have covered the subject matter we had learned in class. At times a student who knew the material was unable to score substantially higher than one who did not, because all too often scoring well was a matter of feeding back to the teacher the answers he wanted—not always the best answers.

Then there were those teachers who graded on the curve, which meant that those who did the best got the "A" and the same number of students received an "F." The same quality of work might merit an "A" in one class, a "C" in another. A student could earn a 90 percent on a paper and still not really be sure if it was good or not. It might have been the highest score in the class—or it could have been the lowest.

You will not have this trouble with IQ tests, because they are **standardized tests.** Basically what that means is that such tests have been given to a large group of people representative of those to whom the tests will be administered in the future. The scores the members of this group make are then fixed in a arbitrary fashion and given meaningful values.

From raw score to standardized score

The raw score is, very simply, the score received on a test. It can be the number of correct answers or, as on some multiple choice tests, the number of correct answers less a percentage of the incorrect answers (to compensate for guessing). **The raw score has no real meaning in itself; it is only when the raw scores are compared that they take on meaning.**

How is this comparison of scores accomplished? The mean (average) test score is determined and it is given an aribtrary value called a **standard score equivalent.** (In the case of IQ, the standard score equivalent is 100.) Then the other raw scores are arranged (fixed) to fit an arbitrary pattern and are also assigned standard values.

It really makes no difference how many items or percent of items are answered correctly when figuring the standard scores. If, for instance, the average score on the test happened to be 22, then a score of 22 on that particular test will be the score from which all the other scores are fixed.

To understand the process by which scores are fixed, you need only an elementary understanding of the statistical device called the Normal Curve of Distribution. You probably know this curve, though perhaps not by this name.

In statistics, it is assumed that many measurements, including scores on a well-constructed test, will fall or are distributed under what is called the normal, or bell-shaped, curve: with most cases falling in the middle, or at the average, and the fewest cases falling at either extreme.

To see how this distribution occurs, we will use a standardized IQ test as an example. Remember that the test has been administered to a large, representative group first, and the questions reflect those abilities the experts have determined to be related to intelligence.

For our exmaple, let us say that the representative group taking this IQ test was made up entirely of six-year-old children. First, the raw scores are determined and the average or mean raw score is found. This mean score, whatever it happens to be, is given an IQ equivalent of 100. In the future, any six-year-old who makes this raw score on this test is said to have an IQ of 100.

To obtain the other IQ values, the remaining raw scores are put in order from lowest to highest. They are then grouped according to the percentages shown in the following illustration of the **normal curve of distribution.**

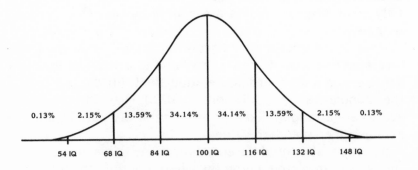

The Normal Curve of Distribution is a pictorial representation of the percentage of cases expected to fall between certain points, in this case IQ scores.

By looking at the illustration, you can see that approximately one-third (34.14%) of the scores will be given IQ values between 100 and 116 in their rank order. Another one-sixth of the scores will be even higher and will be given IQ values according to where they fall along this normal curve of distribution. IQs above 148 are rare and those much above this score are extremely rare and quite difficult to measure.

Other Standard Scores

An IQ score is a standard score; and, as such, it has meaning. It is an arbitrary figure that tells us how well one child performed on one test as compared to how well the large group of children in the standardizing group did when they took this particular test.

After your child has been tested, the results should be explained to you. You might be told your child has an IQ of 137. You can then look at the illustration of the Normal Curve of Distribution and see how this score compares with others. You can tell that an IQ of 137 is in the top two percent.

Whether the IQ is 137, or 138, or 134 is not important. A difference of a few points has little meaning; it could be caused by any number of factors unrelated to intelligence. The thing you want to know is the range within which this IQ falls. It is enough to know that 137 is in the top two percent, because **giftedness must be viewed as a matter of degree rather than as a specific score.**

Another reason minor differences in scores are not important is that there is a margin of error in every test. Statistically, one-third of the IQ scores will be more than seven points in error, just because of test inaccuracy. Since school authorities are aware of the possibility of error in precise IQ scores, they often express the test results in other terms to indicate the range within which they believe special educational provisions should be offered.

Some of these other terms (standard scores) that are frequently used to describe the results of standardized tests are **percentile, stanine,** and **standard deviation.** Before you can have any real idea of what a certain score means, you must know what kind of a score it is, and the most direct way is to

STANDARD SCORES CHART

IQ	STANDARD DEVIATION	STANINE	PERCENTILE
	+ 4		
148	+ 3	9	
			99
132	+ 2		95
		8	90
116	+ 1	7	85
			80
		6	70
			60
100	0	5	50
			40
		4	30
			20
84	− 1	3	15
			10
		2	5
68	− 2		
			1
54	− 3	1	
	− 4		

The relationship among various standard scores.

ask. It is possible though, to figure it out yourself using the Standard Scores Chart shown above, which shows the relationships among the most common standard scores.

If, for example, you were told your child received a "four" on a particular standardized test, you can quickly see it is not likely an IQ score since they do not go that low. It could represent a standard deviation, but if it were it would have either a plus (+) or a minus (−) sign before it: a + 4 being extremely high and a − 4 extremely low. A percentile rank of four would be quite low, meaning that only 4 percent of those taking this test scored lower. A child testing in the fourth stanine would have an IQ a bit below the average.

CRITERION-REFERENCED TESTS

In educational and other testing there is more and more pressure to avoid scores based on comparisons with other test takers; thus arises the popularity of criterion-referenced tests. Because of this pressure, some tests do not use scores standardized on the basis of the normal curve but on the basis of expert judgment of a criterion such as reading readiness or minimum competency. The interpretation of scores or the scores themselves would show readiness or nonreadiness, competency or noncompetency, according to the judgmental criterion rather than according to the scores of other students. Some school systems are moving rapidly toward criterion-referenced tests (CRTs) in all areas including the selection of students for special programs.

CONCLUSION

An IQ test is a very powerful instrument. It can be the key to unlock the doors to educational opportunities for some children whose needs are not being met in the traditional school setting. It can serve as a confirmation of your suspicions about the exceptionality of your child.

If your child scores high on an IQ test, you may rise to the challenge by encouraging the kind of play, hobbies, experiences, and education that will aid in his total development. You could respond by basking in false pride. You could love, accept, and enjoy him in his uniqueness.

Before you agree to the testing of your child, ask yourself these questions:

Can this test tell me something I don't already know?
Will the information be used to help my child?

Only if you can answer in the affirmative to both these questions, and if someone whose opinion you value agrees with you, should you consider an intelligence test for your preschool child.

Superior children seldom differ markedly from their average peers as infants. Your first suspicion of exceptionality might come when you notice your child is unusually persistent and notably more curious than other children, or when language development begins and proceeds at an extraordinary pace. Although the absence of rapid language development does not necessarily mean the absence of superior ability, its presence is often a positive sign. It is through words that we express thoughts and the way a child uses language can give a clue to the quality of the thinking he is employing. The kinds of questions the young talker asks and the complexity of his sentence construction are also indicators. His interests and his choice of companions also serve to confirm your growing suspicions. All of these observations are more reliable than tests at this early age.

There are infant tests whose purpose is to evaluate cognitive development. Since they are heavily weighted in the areas of motor development and attention, their greatest value lies in their recognized ability to detect developmental problems.

As your gifted child reaches school age, identification of giftedness begins to make sense. When he enters school, you have less control over his environment. If his needs are not being met, and if significant changes should be made in his educational environment, IQ tests can function as the proof of his eligibility for special provisions.

Most school systems use a series of screening devices to determine which children will benefit from a special curriculum. Group IQ tests are most often used for this screening, while the more reliable individually administered IQ test is reserved for positive identification.

The results of any IQ test cannot be applied absolutely to any one individual. These instruments are designed to compare the performance of the child taking the test with the performance of a large group on whom the particular test was standardized. The resulting score reflects what a particular child did on a particular test at a particular time.

The problems with IQ testing more often lie in the misinterpretation of the results than in the test itself. Different scores can mean different things. No one test should be the sole determinant for entrance to or exclusion from a certain program of instruction. The person interpreting the results must be familiar with the limitations of the particular test.

Minor differences in scores are not really terribly significant. The child with a 132 IQ is not appreciably different from the one who has a 138 IQ. Both of these children will probably benefit from special educational provisions. However, if you are told that your child had the highest score possible on the test (or on a section of the test) you can be assured that this test (or section) has not adequately assessed his ability. If you are told that his score is 148 + , or an equivalent standard score, you should be aware that his score is extremely rare and few schools are equipped to handle the needs of this child.

The line of demarcation between normal and exceptional is not universally agreed upon. Where along the intellectual continuum does giftedness begin and normalness end? What about the child who is exceptional in one area and quite average, or below, in others? Tests are only one tool to be used in answering these questions.

Educators share your concern about these questions. If the working definition of giftedness is too broad, some children may be included who do not need, or may even be harmed by, the faster pace and competition of a gifted program. On the other hand, a definition that is too exclusive may cause some students who are in great need of special provisions to be missed.

The child who has exceptional intellectual and/or creative thinking ability must be afforded the opportunity to develop into the kind of person who can view himself as worthwhile, capable of reaching self-set goals, and as someone who can form meaningful personal relationships.

13

Questions Parents Ask

Q: **"When do differences in intellectual ability show up?"**

A: Seldom before the onset of walking and talking, and usually later. We cannot judge a child's ultimate capacity on the basis of early performance alone. Piaget liked to point out the differences between animals of just a few weeks and a child of the same age. The animals are so much further advanced than the human infant at this time, yet we know the human will progress much further.

Even though intellectual differences are not so apparent in the first two years, researchers have observed that the kinds of experiences gifted children have appear to be of a higher quality and are more conducive to exceptional growth than the experiences of their average peers.

Q: **"I feel so much pressure to help my child to develop to his full capacity, it makes me nervous. Will I ever get over it?"**

A: Yes, the nervousness will go away when you realize that your goal of developing your child's capacity to the fullest is as unattainable as it is undefinable. It is doubtful if anyone ever develops to his fullest.

Relax. Remember how you used to lie in bed and listen for your baby's breathing? How you could hear it from the other room? You got used to that and you will get used to the idea of parenting a gifted child.

Q: **"I know gifted preschoolers ask lots of questions and that I should answer them. But Daryll asks some that I just can't answer."**

A: Part of a gifted child's mission in life will be to ask the unanswerable—for this is how great truths are discovered. Do not discourage such questions by ignoring them, or by giving long complicated answers or even incorrect ones. Tell Daryll you are not sure, but "maybe we can find out." If you cannot find the answer, he can live with that—some questions have no answers.

Q: **"I sometimes feel guilty that we are not spending more of our time and resources on the development of our child's gifts . . ."**

Q: **"We don't intend to alter our life-style one bit . . ."**

A: Parents frequently have trouble deciding just how much they must adapt their life-style to the needs of their gifted offspring. Effective parenting of a gifted child **is** time-consuming and **does** require some concessions and accommodations, particularly through the early years . . . but **giftedness does not require constant attention.**

I see this problem as analogous to the raising of a fine plant. A seed, with all its own potential to be a rose or a daisy or a dandelion, must be started in the right kind of soil and given the kind of care that will stimulate its peculiar growth pattern. As the plant becomes stronger, it needs less attention and will soon be able to withstand some adverse conditions. Each seedling has its own needs to become the finest rose, daisy, or dandelion possible. Too much sun or water can be just as harmful to the new seedling as too little. The successful gardner knows the difference. The wise gardner appreciates each for its own uniqueness.

Q: "I don't want my little girl thinking she is special just because she is smarter than the other kids in the neighborhood. What can I do about the adults who are always bragging on her?"

A: A little bragging is not going to hurt anyone—in fact it is rather nice. However, if it becomes excessive, as you indicate by your use of the word **always,** I would suggest you speak to the worst offenders. Explain your fears and ask them to stop. If this is not possible, you should talk to your daughter and help her put these compliments into perspective, making sure she does not interpret your concern as a criticism of her gifted behavior.

Q: "Our older son is gifted and he began having emotional problems when he entered school. We are worried that our three-year-old daughter will be similarly troubled if she goes to the same school. What should we do?"

A: Gifted children are not immune from various emotional or behavioral problems. Although these problems may be noticed early by a parent who is aware of what is normal for the gifted, negative tendencies frequently do not appear until children enter school. It would be unwise to assume that the teacher or the educational program is necessarily the cause of these disturbances simply because of the timing of their emergence. Changing schools or teachers might not be the solution. These potentially serious problems could be more than a school guidance counselor is equipped to handle and might require the attention of a psychologist.

Q: "I have been reading that the gifted have severe emotional problems when they reach adolescence. Is this true?"

A: Social insecurity is natural in adolescence and is heightened in the gifted because of their keen perception and their acute sensitivity. They can and frequently do experience intense emotional pain at this age. However, the superior intelligence, which may contribute to the pain, is often that which helps them to overcome it in the end.

Q: "We are having a problem with Kevin's playschool teacher. She expects so much of him. No matter how good his efforts are, she always finds fault. When he does something naughty, she acts as if she expected it and tells us, in front of him, that if he were really smart he wouldn't do it. She tells us the trouble with parents of gifted children is they don't expect enough of them."

A: She is wrong. Get Kevin out of that school—now.

Q: "So many children seem to start some sort of pre-school when they are three and they seem to learn so much. Am I hurting my daughter by keeping her at home this year?"

A: Probably not. I doubt that your daughter would learn much at nursery school that she could not learn equally well, or better, at home.

There is a side to this question that you really ought to consider. By age three, most children are ready and eager for peer interaction. To deprive your daughter of any opportunity to be with other children would not be wise. She also needs occasional experiences under the care of an adult authority other than her parents.

Q: "Our four-year-old grandson is coming to stay with us for a week this summer. He is gifted and loves books. I want to buy a selection for him to read while he is here. What do you suggest?"

A: You have a wonderful opportunity to open up new worlds to your grandchild through the selection you make. My suggestion would be for you to purchase several beautifully illustrated books on a variety of topics that interest you. Share these with your grandson. Your enthusiasm will be contagious.

Haunt the used book stores, garage sales, or bazaars for books about animals, insects, dinosaurs, the microscopic world, sea life, plants, the wonders of nature; and don't forget poetry and the classics. These books are usually expensive, but they last forever and have so much to interest the child. Read them to him, discuss the pictures, and give him time alone to pour over them. He will probably look forward to curling up with these favorites every time he comes to visit.

Q: "My child has been chosen for the gifted program at his school, and I am having mixed feelings about it. How can I determine if the program will be to his benefit?"

A: First, find out as much about the program as you can:

use the checklist in Chapter 11 and decide if it is a good program. Then, take a look at your child: Can he take the pressures and the competition inherent in a gifted program? Is his self-concept strong enough that he will be comfortable as an average student in a gifted group? Does this program offer more, not only intellectual stimulation, but also social contacts and emotional outlets than he has now? Finally, if everything else seems right, go ahead and let him try it.

Q: **"My child doesn't want to go into the gifted program. I really think it will be good for him. Shall I make him go?"**

A: That is a decision you will have to make. I can only tell you that I have spoken to many gifted children who strongly resisted the move into a gifted program; but said once they were enrolled they were never happier.

Q: **"I read in a popular Sunday supplement that 30 percent of high school dropouts are gifted. I was horrified! What can we do?"**

A: I was horrified too, but I do not believe it. The figures just do not add up.

Take an average high school with an enrollment of 2,000 students, 40 to 50 of whom are gifted (2–2.5 percent). Using a dropout rate of 20 percent, you would expect 400 of the students to drop out. If 30 percent of the 400 dropouts were gifted, as the article claimed, it would mean that 120 of the dropouts were gifted. That is more than twice the total number of gifted in the school. Common sense tells me this is ridiculous.

In 1962, Donald Green studied the dropout rate in the Iowa high schools and found that 17.6 percent of the gifted students left before graduation. Using our sample school of 2,000, we might expect eight or nine of the 40 to 50 gifted students to drop out. While the rate may differ in other parts of the country, these figures are believable.

Even eight or nine gifted dropouts are not to be ignored, especially if one of these is your child. There are things we can do to lower the rate: offer educational programs to meet the needs of the gifted, make good counseling available to them, and give each child a good foundation in his preschool years in the home.

Q: "Are there particular kinds of games and/or toys (besides books) that are recommended as gifts for gifted preschoolers?"

A: This can be a problem because the suggested age levels on games and toys are seldom appropriate for gifted children, and it is hard to get assistance from the salesperson because **every** grandmother says hers is a gifted child (the difference is, yours is). Probably the best way to find a toy or game your gifted grandchild will enjoy is to get the names of his favorites so you will know the kinds of things he enjoys. With this clue, the salesperson should be able to make suggestions from which you can choose the one you prefer.

Look for games and toys with a variety of uses, which encourage creativity or present some sort of challenge. Parquet blocks are good because so many things can be done with them and at so many different conceptual levels: learn about colors and shapes, build with them, make and copy patterns. Giant cardboard building bricks, take apart and put together toys, and Lego or Tinker Toys are favorites. Gifted preschoolers also like games they can play with adults, with some chance of winning, such as variations of Lotto or Concentration.

Q: "My five-year-old is so advanced, I find myself expecting adult-like behavior all the time."

A: We all do. On first meeting a precocious child we usually find ourselves surprised by his advanced speech and his poise. Then, when he occasionally lapses into perfectly normal behavior, we are almost always surprised. These expectations can be rather hard on a child who, most of the time, really wants to be treated as if he is much older, yet is never to be allowed to act like a five-year-old.

Q: "Do you think it is absolutely necessary for a mother to stay home from work when the kids are small? I don't think it matters how much time I spend with my baby—it is the quality of the time we spend together that counts."

A: No, I do not think it is absolutely necessary for the mother to stay home; father can do an equally effective job of nurturing. If it is impossible for either of you to be with your child during most of his waking hours, then it is vital that you be very selective about the person chosen to act as your substitute during the critical, first few years of your baby's life.

As for quality versus quantity of time: There is no question that top quality parenting is always preferable. This does not negate the fact that your child is learning **something** between those quality periods! Your very young child is absorbing enormous amounts of information constantly during his waking hours and, since he cannot reach beyond his environment, what he hears about life and his place in the world will be determined by the person you choose to control his environment when you are not around.

Q: **"Aaron is such a quiet child, I worry that he won't be able to handle himself in a rough-and-tumble group of peers."**

A: Aaron will be better equipped to handle himself in **any** group if he has the opportunity to learn how to get along with others. Begin gradually working him into group situations, now. Start with small groups of two to three children whom he knows, and eventually work up to groups of as many as eight to ten children of whom he knows only one or two. Take your time, making sure his first attempts at group interactions are successful ones. He is sharp; he will learn.

Q: **"In our country it is the practice to push the gifted students ahead. When is the best time to skip grades? My daughter just entered kindergarten and they want to skip her into first grade. Should I go along with this idea?"**

A: The schools seldom suggest that a youngster skip kindergarten unless they are convinced the child would be better off in the first grade. This is an ideal time for a precocious child to move ahead. So, unless you can think of some reason why your daughter should not, I would give approval to the move, if I were you.

Beginning school a year early has been proved a good idea for many bright, mature youngsters. They usually adapt easily and keep up with the class (and often move ahead of it) and are spared the tedium of a year in an unmotivating kindergarten.

After entering school early, the easiest times to skip grades are just before changing schools. In most areas, this would mean skipping sixth, ninth, and/or twelfth grades.

Q: **"Kelly is an extremely gifted mathematician, but seems quite average in all other academic subjects. Will it be possible for him to score high enough on an IQ test to be eligible for special education?"**

A: In order to score high on an intelligence test, Kelly must either do well in all the subtests, or tremendously well in one. Kelly's ability is so outstanding there is little doubt it will be made apparent in the testing.

Q: **"Do you encourage going beyond his years in particular areas if the child shows an exceptional interest? If so, how do you go about finding what his limitations are?"**

A: Yes, gifted children by definition go beyond their years—it is really very hard to hold them back in areas of exceptional interest. The gifted let you know when they reach their limits. Even the highly gifted, with whom the sky is the limit, reach plateaus caused either by immaturity or the need for practice.

If it is encouragement and opportunity you offer your child, there is little danger of pushing him past his "limits." As far as his ultimate limitations are concerned, there is no way you, or anyone else, can tell that now. Too much is involved in the fulfillment of potential to be able to predict with accuracy just how far any one child will go.

Q: **"Isn't there the possibility that if a preschooler learns to read she will be bored when she goes to school?"**

A: Yes, a reader may be bored . . . but then so might a nonreader.

Q: **"Our daughter is gifted, but she is so clumsy. My husband says that's the way gifted children are because they have so much on their minds. Is this so?"**

A: Some gifted children are clumsy, and some are just careless. But **most** children, gifted or not, would rather be graceful or be skilled in a sport. It is important to a child's self-image, and therefore should receive parental attention.

Why don't you arrange for your daughter to take dancing lessons or gymnastics, or see that she participates in some sporting activity in which she has a chance of becoming proficient?

Q: "What are the chances that my gifted child will be a happy adult?"

A: The odds are heavily weighted in his favor.

Q: "In my high school years, most of the best students were standoffish and uppity because they thought they were so smart. We don't ever use that word (smart) around Nancy. We don't want her to think she's better than her playmates, and we are afraid she will tell them we think she is smarter than they."

A: There is one fact you and Nancy will, sooner or later, have to face: **she is smart.** We all tell our children they are beautiful and smart and good and funny and cute and loveable. I cannot see any reason not to, just because it happens to be true. By consciously omitting praise for a part of Nancy's being, you might be conveying to her the message that her brightness is a source of embarrassment to you. There will be times—maybe many times—when Nancy will have doubts about her intellectual capacity. If she cannot go to you for reassurance, to whom could she turn?

You cannot help how others view your child, but you can influence how she views herself and how she presents herself to others. Teach her to be considerate of others and to view her giftedness as just one part—and a good one—of her wholeness.

Q: "Why do so many of today's gifted children seem to need help with reading problems? Even our school's LD (Learning Disabilities) teacher has some gifted children in her classes."

A: There are almost as many reasons for a student to have reading problems as there are students who have them. I am not convinced that the gifted have any more reading problems than before. I suspect that we are seeing more of them because, now, we are able to recognize giftedness in a child who cannot read well, whereas previously we seldom identified a nonreader as gifted.

Q: "What children's TV shows do you recommend?"

A: I find that most of the programs aired for children are much too stimulating for the preschooler and the materials taught could be better learned in other ways. Some science and nature programs, intended for family viewing, can open up a world of experience not otherwise accessible to most children.

Use your television guide and be selective about the programs you permit your preschooler to watch. Watch them with him and observe his reactions. If the program is not up to your expectations, turn the set off and go on to some more valuable use of your time. If the subject matter of the program is controversial, discuss it with your child, giving him the viewpoint you want stressed.

Q: **"What do you think about TV?"**

A: The best thing about television is that you can turn it off, particularly if there is a preschooler in the house. No matter how valuable the program appears to be, you should ask yourself, before turning the set on, if your preschooler can take this precious time away from other experiences and activities that can teach the social, intellectual, and physical skills basic to a meaningful life.

Q: **"It worries me; my child is brighter than his father. How should I handle this?"**

A: I do not see that this, in itself, will be the cause of any great problem. The gifted are brighter than **most** people. The problem will come if your child does not learn to respect other people for their various qualities, not only exceptional intelligence. Your husband has much to offer your child, including knowledge born of experience and the wisdom of years.

All children think they are smarter than their parents at one time or another. If some weren't, our civilization would revert to the Stone Age.

Q: **"I have a bright child who is quite inactive. How can I motivate him to get out and play like other kids? I am afraid he is not developing social skills. Should I even be concerned?"**

A: Yes, you should be concerned if you believe your child is not developing the important social skills. He may be avoiding the kinds of outdoor games the other children are playing because he is not proficient at them, or it may be that he is just not interested in the games they are playing. Do not overlook all the opportunities for learning social skills through other, less active pursuits—the kinds your son prefers. He is more likely to be successful in his early attempts at socializing when he is engaged in an activity he enjoys.

There are other reasons for a young person to "get out and play." One is his need for exercise. You can encourage your bright child to be more active by offering him some sort of lessons or by taking up a sport, such as jogging, as a family. If exercise is the goal, be realistic; he will probably get more exercise walking through a museum than he will get sitting on the bench in a softball game.

Q: **"What do you think of the workbooks for preschoolers that are sold in magazine racks and at the bookstores? Is it all right to buy them for my child?"**

A: There is some real junk on the market, yet some of the workbooks I have seen are really very good and fun to work. You cannot always go by the publisher's name or the author's reputation. You must be the judge of a workbook's quality and appropriateness for your child. If the title is something like **Phonics Fun for Preschoolers,** open it up and see if the activities really are fun—sometimes they are mere drudgery! Look for some continuity in the types of activities so a child, after being told how to do one or two pages, can find other similar pages and proceed on his own. Look, also, for enough variety to make the book interesting.

If your child enjoys working with these books, go ahead. If your choices are made selectively and critically, she ought to learn something from them. Help her when she needs help, keep it fun, and please do not make her work every page from cover to cover.

Q: **"We are trying to increase our child's vocabulary by using synonyms and more precise words when we speak to her, but she does not seem to get the fine distinctions. It is really very frustrating. Should we stop?"**

A: Do you remember when she called every man "Daddy?" It really did not take long for her to discover that all men were not daddy. Give her time and, with your patient help, she will soon be able to discriminate the finer meanings in the words you use.

No, you need not stop this practice; you must only make sure she understands the general concept before you proceed. For example, you cannot expect her to use the words "oriole," "robin," or "eagle" until she is first sure about the meaning of the word "bird." Then, when she points out a bird, you can say something to help her notice the qualities that make this one different from the others, such as, "Yes, that **red** bird is a **cardinal**."

Q: **"There is a twelve-year-old boy in our building who has an IQ of 206. Is he a genius?"**

A: The meaning of any IQ score is obscure unless we know how the score was obtained. A score of 206—which is certainly at the top of the genius range—is impossible to reach on the most widely used and respected tests: the Wechsler and the Stanford-Binet (see Chapter 12). Perhaps an estimate was made of this boy's unusual ability. Even then, at six points higher than the score Leta Hollingworth described as the "topmost limits of human diversity," it seems to be an exaggeration.

Q: **"What can I do about grandparents who are always correcting the children's grammar?"**

A: Explain to the grandparents that young children learn the proper use of their language through hearing it used, rather than through correction. If they are concerned about the children's grammar, tell them that their efforts will be far more effective if they make careful use of proper grammar around them and see that others do the same. You, and they, should really be more concerned with what your children are trying to communicate at this age than with how they are saying it. Later, there will certainly be times when correction will be necessary, and beneficial.

Q: **"I saw a television program about toddlers being taught to read aloud the names of foreign countries and find them on a map. Is this possible?"**

A: Yes, and I have seen chickens trained to peck out a tune on a piano.

When we teach a child to read, it is our goal for him to react mentally to the printed word. Whatever method he uses to unlock the pronunciation of printed symbols, in the long run the essential ingredient in the reading process is that which goes on in the head, not what comes out of the mouth. For example, some languages are much more phonetic than English, making them far easier to pronounce. While I might find it a simple task to "read" a passage in Spanish, I may have no idea at all what the passage is saying. By the same token, a student could "read" a passage from Hamlet, yet have no comprehension of its meaning at all.

The toddler who reads the word AFGHANISTAN, can hardly have the reaction to those letters that another young reader would have in reading the word CIRCUS, especially had the latter been to a circus at one time.

If your preschooler has a broad experiential background and has built a large speaking vocabulary, he will be more likely to comprehend the messages in printed words when he does begin to read.

Q: **"Whenever our daughter or son asks us a question, we make them figure the answer out for themselves. Do you think this is a good idea?"**

A: It is a great idea when done with discretion. We have to figure out some things for ourselves, and when we do, we usually get a good deal of satisfaction and learning in the process. Sometimes, though, it is more efficient to have someone just tell us quickly what we want to know. When, for example, your child is deeply involved in writing a story and wants to know how to spell a word, it is not the time to stop his creative work for a spelling lesson. Tell him the word, and work in the spelling lesson later.

Q: **"What should I do if my child flunks the IQ test to qualify for the gifted program?"**

A: First of all, one does not "flunk" an IQ test. The schools, of necessity, must honor some cutoff score for determining who will be eligible for inclusion in their special programs. If you child fails to score above this arbitrary point, it does not necessarily mean that he is not gifted. As John Merrow said, "Unfortunately, intelligence and talent, like beauty, are often in the eye of the beholder."

If your child does not qualify as gifted according to his school's policy, tell him, not that he flunked, but that the test results show he does not need this particular program to do well in school. It is most probable that his educational needs **will** be met just as well, or maybe even better, in a regular classroom where he will not experience the pressure of trying to compete with a roomful of gifted peers.

When your child comes out of the testing room, he has not changed. He is the same child who entered an hour before. It is so important that you convey to him in both words and actions that your high opinion of him and good feelings toward him have not been altered, regardless of the results of the test.

14

The Last Word

I would like to share with you the views of some other people who have already been where you and your child are now. I asked a number of parents, whose gifted children are now well past the preschool age, what advice they would give a parent just starting out, and I also asked some gifted young people what **they** thought a parent should know. Their replies are recorded here.

THE PARENTS SPEAK

"I feel that gifted children have basically the same requirements as any child. I believe their parents, like all parents, have the responsibility to learn parenting skills."

"Parents should be informed 1) of the importance of fostering and supporting the natural questioning and probing of their child, 2) that their precocious children are still children—their need for affection and guidance (firm, reasonable, well-defined limits) is as great or greater than 'average' children."

"I feel the concept of raising a 'competent' child, one who is able to make decisions wisely, who has a strong self-concept, and who is happy and at ease, is especially important when raising a gifted child."

"Use common sense. Share experiences with other parents. Read what the experts have to say."

"Adjustment to their relationship with other kids who seem 'dumb' . . . it's impatience rather than snobbishness. Be careful not to give them too much responsibility too fast just because they are adult intellectually."

"Gifted children make parenting easy. Family reads books and discusses things, so they just do the same. They are natural leaders so have many friends."

"It is important that they receive the best education possible while remaining well-rounded children."

"Expect emotional upsets as the child may be frustrated with everyday life on the level of her age group."

"Do not pressure a gifted child toward academics, some preschool mothers are intent upon their child developing in this area when the youngster needs social growth, the ability to play with other preschoolers. Mothers often emphasize the cerebral gifts of their children and ignore the fact that her youngster is socially behaving in ways that are not accepted. Seek to produce positive goals in these areas as well. They are as important as pouring skills into a preschool child."

"Introduce as much information and opportunities as possible. Start early. Make it fun, not school."

"Very often it seems that gifted people recognize—and perhaps accurately—that they need not expend much effort to accomplish goals and so never learn to achieve what they might if they met early and consistent challenges. We believe it very important for our gifted children to recognize the moral obligation they have to develop their potentials."

And finally one parent stated simply:

"Gifted children can wear you out."

THE GIFTED CHILD'S VIEW

The following are the opinions of a number of gifted boys and girls, ranging in age from eight to eighteen. All of these students have been identified as gifted (IQ 132 +) and many attend a special school for the gifted. Although these children can be profound, they are far from perfect—as their quite ordinary spelling and grammar reveal.

On Being Gifted

"It's not how smart you are, it's what you do that counts."

"My parents make me mad by thinking I'm perfect and can do anything at all. They yell at me a lot, and expect me to do **everything."**

"It's hard enough being bright without someone broadcasting it."

"Parents must not feel threatened by it [intelligence]. The feelings of my parents make me feel guilty and defensive about anything 'cerebral' I do."

"When I learned I was a gifted student I was happy and I new I was smart and I could read write and it is just great."

"Most of the students who are 'gifted' are assumed to be motivated—not true."

"When I was idintified as gifted I was surprised."

"My parents let me do alot of things I don't think I'd be able to do if I wasn't gifted."

"I'm sure my parents trust me more since I'm gifted than if I wasn't."

"I feel good because I am a gifted child."

"It's neat and will make me what I want to be—a space technoligist."

"They are just like any other kid except that their brains are more 'worked on' when they're kids."

"Gifted children are sometimes not children at all."

On Attending a School for the Gifted:

"When I found out I was gifted and going to this school, it felt like I didn't have any friends anymore but, then it felt like I had all the friends in the universe."

"I felt very happy and excited but I was afraid of this school."

"Everybody that I tell say I'm a Big shot, so I'd feel alot happier if it wasn't a school for the gifted."

"Everytime my mother meets someone new—she tells them I go to a school for the gifted. Maybe she thinks they'll think **she's** smart. I think that's dumb!"

On Responsibility and Encouragement:

"The more parents push, the more responsibility they take from the child."

"See what the child is most interested in, and encourage it, but don't push it. Some parents push too much in one direction, which leads to discouragement."

"My parents make me happy by encouraging me to do good work."

"I wish they, my parents, wouldn't yell and tell me not to do something, then go off and do it thimselves."

"Commend the child on good work, do not bribe them. Let the kid do it out of his/her own initiative."

"Give them **some** responsibilities, but ask them if they think it is to much or if they can handle more."

"I wish my parents wouldn't tell me what to do when I alredy know what I have to do. Then they yell at me until I finish."

"Don't nag about homework. Parents can assist, but kids have to realize that the responsibility is theirs."

"Children should be encouraged to take responsibilities."

"Give them responsiblities, they will become independant."

On Decision-Making:

"Let the child make decisions."

"Parents don't seem to give their kids enough credit for the kids's intelligence and good judgement. My parents have left a lot of decisions to me, and I feel that I have made the right decisions most of the time. I think this helps children mature faster and improve the child's self-confidence."

"I think it's important not to influence a child too much, but to let him make his own choices."

"Don't worry about the little things. It won't hurt us to make some mistakes."

"Listen to the child and when they have an idea or make a suggestion take them seriously because the chances are that the idea is probably a good one. If you do not think the idea is good tell the child why and explain to he/she how it could be improved."

"I would let my child go on by herself (himself) but sometimes I would check up on them."

"I would set some guidelines, but I would tend to be more lenient as my child matures and is capable of making his/her own decisions."

"Don't be an overprotective parent, it only makes kids want to do things more."

On Parenting a Gifted Child:

"I think parents should answer their children's questions, let them use their own judgement, listen to them, spend time with them but also give them time away from you, read to them and encourage them to learn, expose them to many different forms of art and music. Let them know you love them, are proud of them."

"My parents make me happy when they have talks with me!"

"Please tell them not to live through their children. My mother tells everyone who will listen my test scores or my grades. I've always felt the pressure to do well."

"Instill into them certain traits: discipline, punctuality, responsibility, respect, etc., as soon as possible. These, I believe, are very important traits. I would also expose him to good manners."

"My parents make me smarter by telling me if my anwer is wrong but don't tell me what the answer is."

"One of the **most** important things is for a parent to spend individual time with their child . . . for instance: reading."

"Let them know you love them."

"Parents of gifted pre-schoolers should be careful not to curtail their children's creativity. While doing this, however, they should not spare any needed discipline in the name of advancing their child's creativity."

"Parents should give him or her lots of oppurtournities :

fishing,

snorkeling,

camping,

skiing,

just fun."

"I have observed a well reknowned theory to be true: children tend to become what one tells them they are, so be positive and encouraging."

"Don't get worried about every little thing that happens to them."

"If I were a parent, I would always tell my children that I shall listen to them—**no matter what!** That they can always come to me with their problems. I shall also reprimand them according to their misbehavior."

"Expose them to various things in their world and explain, in their own 'type of language,' how it works or how it benefits us. Don't get **too** technical but expand their knowledge of the world about them."

"Show love and affection, be there when the child needs them, and have respect for the child's feelings."

"Treat them well but don't spoil them."

"I believe that my early childhood included several factors that inspired my desire to learn. These factors, instilled by both parents included: answering my questions with a serious attitude, reading books out loud, and respecting my thoughts and views, whatever they might have been."

"My parents yell at me a lot because I'm slow. I wish they wouldn't."

"When raising a gifted child one should try to understand that their child is different and should realize that the child's actions will not always reflect their age and will sometimes be an inconvenience."

"The parents set the example."

"My parents made me feel good about myself which built up my self-confidence. Now as I'm ready to enter college, I have high goals and a good, positive feeling about the new experiences."

ONE LAST WORD

You have the good fortune to be raising a very special child. You probably have sufficient knowledge, ability, and desire to be a successful parent; and, I am sure, you are well aware of the great responsibility that is yours. You know your child has all the nurturing needs of any child—and then some!

In this handbook I have given you an overview of the most important information you should need concerning gifted children and the factors affecting their development. You have just read what some gifted children view as important, and the advice of parents who have gone through the same experiences you are having now. They made it—some over rockier roads than others, some with more success than others—but they did it, and so can you.

Now, before wishing you well on your parenting venture, I want to add one final word, a simple word of caution. Consider the suggestions and the information given in this book, and any other book for that matter, in the light of **your own good sense of what is right for you and for your own child.** Trust your judgment. Although you have some things in common with other parents, you are like no other, just as your child is not like all other gifted children.

You **should** have high expectations for your gifted child, but they must be consistent with your knowledge of his needs, ability, and stage of development. Take your cues from him. Listen to him; watch him. But do not assume that you can always infer or intuit what your child is thinking or feeling—no matter how sensitive or how knowledgeable a parent you may be. Sometimes you must ask; and if your child has learned early in life that you care and will listen, he is likely to communicate with you now and later.

Your child will undoubtedly require a certain amount of "pushing," but this must be tempered with an understanding on your part that **a gifted child seldom feels that he has done his best.** When he needs help, give it to him. Only you can decide how much help to offer, and when. He needs praise for a job well done; but he will recognize, and perhaps resent, insincere praise.

You do not spoil a child with care; you spoil him with neglect. A caring parent provides a certain amount of structure, guidelines for behavior, encouragement, freedom within limits, respect, values, responsibility, guidance, models, and love.

A neglected child is not taught self-control, does not have a sense of personal worth. The parents who say to their child, "Do whatever you want" or "Be whatever you want" are really telling him that they do not care what he does or what he becomes. Neglectful parents do not take the time to set consistent guidelines and limits or to listen with enough sensitivity to know when to keep "hands off."

The roots of all human development must be carefully tended and given room to grow in a nurturing environment. Wings of independence must be tested again and again before an individual can soar on his own.